Created for Love

Created for Love

*Towards a New Teaching on
Sex and Marriage*

Edited by
Theo Hobson
and
John Inge

CANTERBURY
PRESS

© The Editors and Contributors 2025

Published in 2025 by the Canterbury Press Norwich

Editorial office
3rd Floor, Invicta House,
110 Golden Lane,
London EC1Y 0TG, UK
www.canterburypress.co.uk

Canterbury Press is an imprint of Hymns Ancient & Modern Ltd
(a registered charity)

Hymns Ancient & Modern® is a registered trademark of
Hymns Ancient & Modern Ltd
13A Hellesdon Park Road, Norwich,
Norfolk NR6 5DR, UK

All rights reserved. No part of this publication may be reproduced,
stored in a retrieval system, or transmitted,
in any form or by any means, electronic, mechanical,
photocopying or otherwise, without the prior permission of
the publisher, Canterbury Press.

The editors and contributors have asserted their right under the Copyright,
Designs and Patents Act 1988 to be identified as the Author of this Work

Scripture quotations are from New Revised Standard Version Bible: Anglicized
Edition, copyright © 1989, 1995 National Council of the Churches of Christ in
the United States of America. Used by permission. All rights reserved worldwide.

British Library Cataloguing in Publication data
A catalogue record for this book is available
from the British Library

ISBN: 978 1-78622-669-3

EU GPSR Authorised Representative
LOGOS EUROPE, 9 rue Nicolas Poussin, 17000, LA ROCHELLE, France
E-mail: Contact@logoseurope.eu

No part of this book may be used or reproduced in any manner for the
purpose of training artificial intelligence technologies or systems.

Typeset by Regent Typesetting

Contents

The Contributors vii
Introduction: A Dialogue xi

Part 1 Bible

1 Beyond Patriarchy: Scripture and Tradition 3
  Miranda Threlfall-Holmes

2 Holy Wedlock and Intimate God: A Biblical Teaching
  of Marriage 13
  Barnabas Palfrey

Part 2 Church

3 Living Well with Difference: A Primer in Anglican
  Ecclesiology 27
  Steven Croft

4 'In Christ' 37
  John Inge

Part 3 Creation

5 Kingdom-shaped Love 49
  Olivia Graham

6 You Made Me This Way Because You Wanted One
  Like Me: Reflections on Sexuality and Creation 61
  Samuel Wells

Part 4 Culture

7 Living in Love and Faith: The Failure of History — 75
  Mark Chapman

8 Dare We Hold Together? — 87
  Vivienne Faull

Part 5 Experience and Conscience

9 Sex Is Not a Dirty Thing: Living in Love and Faith with Maude Royden — 97
  Helen King

10 Time for Change — 109
  Gareth Wardell

Part 6 Prayer and Guidance

11 Created in the Image and Likeness of God: Or Are We? — 119
  Charlie Bell

12 Towards a Unified Theory of Sexual Morality — 129
  Theo Hobson

The Contributors

Charlie Bell is a Church of England priest and a forensic psychiatrist, Scholar in Residence at the Cathedral of St John the Divine in New York, and the Fellow in Medicine and Public Theology at Girton College, Cambridge. He is Associate Vicar at St John the Divine, Kennington.

Mark Chapman is Professor of the History of Modern Theology at the University of Oxford, Distinguished Fellow of Ripon College Cuddesdon, and Canon Theologian of Truro Cathedral. He is a prolific author who has published on many different aspects of the history of the church and theology in the nineteenth and twentieth centuries.

Steven Croft became the Bishop of Oxford in 2016. He spent 13 years in parish ministry in Enfield and Halifax before becoming Warden of Cranmer Hall in 1996, Archbishops Missioner in 2004, and Bishop of Sheffield in 2009. He has written extensively on themes of discipleship, mission and ministry.

Viv Faull has rejoiced in being part of diverse church communities in parishes, a chaplaincy, four cathedrals, and as the Bishop of the Diocese of Bristol until autumn 2025. Her experience of growing up in a church that would not ordain women sensitized her to others who are marginalized by the church's thinking and behaviour, and to those who have internalized that rejection. She has worked for the full inclusion of those in same-sex relationships at every level in the life of the church.

Olivia Graham had a career in international development in Africa before her ordination in 1997. Having served as a parish priest, parish development advisor and archdeacon, she retired as Bishop of Reading in 2024. She has worked on environmental and social justice issues throughout her ministry, and served on General Synod during the *Living in Love and Faith* debates.

Theo Hobson is a freelance writer on religious affairs and a regular contributor to the *Spectator* and the *Tablet*. He has written seven books, mostly on the Church of England and the history of ideas. He also writes about art and religion but prefers trying to make religious art.

John Inge spent 17 years as the 113th Bishop of Worcester prior to his retirement in 2024. Before that he held a variety of ministerial posts including Chaplain of Harrow School, Vicar of a parish in the heart of inner-city Tyneside, Canon Missioner at Ely Cathedral, and Bishop of Huntingdon. His first degree was in chemistry, which he taught prior to ordination. His particular academic interest is in the theology of place.

Helen King is Professor Emerita of Classical Studies at The Open University. A historian of medicine and the body, she is an elected member of General Synod for the Diocese of Oxford, and has served as a trustee of Women and the Church (WATCH) and Together for the Church of England.

Barnabas Palfrey teaches doctrine, ethics and spirituality at St Augustine's College of Theology in London and Kent. He is co-editor with Andreas Telser of *Beyond the Analogical Imagination: The Theological and Cultural Vision of David Tracy* (CUP, 2023), and also with Telser, Langner-Pitschmann, Pittl and Trawöger of *Breaking Boundaries in Theology: In Conversation with Roger Haight SJ* (BRILL, 2025).

THE CONTRIBUTORS

Miranda Threlfall-Holmes is Archdeacon of Liverpool and a member of the Church of England's General Synod and Archbishops' Council. She is author of seven books in the fields of history, ministry and spirituality, most recently *How to Read the Bible: 21 Ways to Enjoy and Understand Scripture* (Hodder & Stoughton, 2024). She blogs on Christianity, history and feminism at mirandathrelfallholmes.blogspot.com.

Gareth Wardell is Vicar of the Parish of St Clement and St James in Kensington, London, in which Grenfell Tower is located. He served with a Christian development agency in Nepal and Afghanistan for nearly 15 years. On returning to the UK, he worked as Research Fellow in the Post-war Reconstruction and Development Unit at York University for several years, before training for ordained ministry at Ridley Hall, Cambridge. He was ordained in York Minister and served his curacy at Selby Abbey before moving to the Diocese of London.

Samuel Wells writes, speaks, preaches and broadcasts on a range of pastoral, political and theological issues. Since 2012 he has been Vicar of St Martin-in-the-Fields, Trafalgar Square, London. St Martin is a unique configuration of commercial, charitable and cultural initiatives rooted in a vibrant congregational life. He is also Visiting Professor of Christian Ethics at King's College London. He has published 50 books.

Introduction: A Dialogue

Theo: This book originated over a cup of tea. I had emailed you, suggesting a chat about the interminable wranglings in Synod over sexuality. It was the spring of 2024, so we'd already seen over a year of Synod debating Living in Love and Faith.[1] For the uninitiated, we should explain that this was a six-year process to look into the question of sexuality and marriage, which at its conclusion proposed significant reform (though to outsiders it might seem rather little): that the Church should offer blessings to same-sex couples.

John: We had a good meeting, and agreed that it was time for those who yearned for the Church of England to take a more inclusive view to take the initiative, having seemingly been on the back foot for too long. Many of us felt as though processes were being used as delaying or blocking tactics, and that very similar arguments to those used before the ordination of female bishops were now being used to stymie progress – change in doctrine, departure from 'biblical truth', fear of schism, ecumenical repercussions, etc. In fact, the sky had not fallen in when female bishops had been ordained. Rather, it enabled the Church of England to present a much more attractive face to the world – as well as benefit from the ministry of some extremely able and effective female bishops.

Theo: I felt dismayed by the recent Synod debate – another dose of clichéd rhetoric on both sides. It seemed annoying that thoughtful reflection was crowded out by the carefully diplomatic language of the archbishops – and also by the predictable rhetoric of the campaigners, by the sheer weight of detail about Resolutions X and Y, by the publishing of the legal advice, and so on – and the big picture was getting lost. On the other hand, I knew that there was an appetite for greater honesty. I interviewed Steven Croft [the Bishop of Oxford] for an article, and was impressed by his candour in advocating same-sex marriage, and his desire to deepen the conversation. I saw that you had also advocated same-sex marriage – I think you were the only other diocesan bishop to do so.

John: I had not said much during the LLF process as bishops of the Church of England had been asked to hold the process of reflection, learning and discernment, rather than express our own views. In November 2022, however, when the process was reaching its conclusion after several years, my colleague the Bishop of Dudley and I wrote an open letter[2] making our own beliefs and hopes plain and supporting the Bishop of Oxford and his reasoning set out in *Together in Love and Faith: Personal Reflections and Next Steps for the Church*, which he had published a day or two previously.[3] I wrote a subsequent open letter giving a theological justification for my approach.[4] It was generally well received but, despite a clear majority of bishops being in favour of change, no progress had been made.

Theo: Let's take a step back and say something about our engagement with the issue prior to LLF – which is complicated by defining what the 'issue' is, or was. Same-sex marriage was hardly even thought about when I started pondering the wider issue of sexuality in the 1990s. I was always vaguely liberal on the issue but, as a heterosexual with some fairly conservative instincts, I was on the fence about the way forward. To be honest, it irked me a bit that the issue came to dominate liberal Anglicanism, especially in the 2000s. Some of the campaigning rhetoric seemed over-the-top, a bit factional and self-righteous. I think the average liberal-ish Anglican just wanted the issue to go away – let's hope it's solved if we allow gay people to be priests and bishops. That was the issue then. But of course the goalposts began to move.

INTRODUCTION

John: My own background is as a liberal catholic Anglican and I had never seen the need to prohibit love between people of the same sex. I had always been haunted by the question attributed to E. M. Forster: 'Is there sufficient love in the world that we can afford to try to stamp out that which there is?' The way the ordination of female priests and bishops had torn apart the catholic movement of the Church of England saddened me, however, and I worried when the equally divisive issue of sexuality began to dominate the agenda and threaten unity. Then came the introduction of same-sex marriage, which blew apart a fragile truce within Anglicanism. As Rowan Williams observed at the time, I believed that the notion of gay marriage was a category error. As time went by, however, I began to reassess to the point where, as I wrote in the open letter above, I believed the Church of England should offer same-sex marriage.

Theo: Yes, I was uneasy when same-sex marriage came in so quickly – just a few years after being mooted, it seemed. The definition of marriage had always been something that Church and State pretty much agreed on, and this felt like secular unilateralism. Suddenly the established Church was awkwardly at odds with the moral and legal consensus, which made its decision more difficult than ever. Reform now looked like following the spirit of the age. So the stakes were raised in the 2010s, and the Church was probably right to start a lengthy consultation process, to take stock.

John: Yes, the LLF process was a brave attempt to enable people of opposing views to communicate respectfully with one another, but it did not enable resolution or reconciliation. I became frustrated that in the 20 years I had been a bishop the Church of England had made no progress – if anything, it had become more conservative. I felt this to be not only an insult to gay people but also a missionary disaster. I became convinced that those of us who wanted to promote a more inclusive approach needed to speak up.

Theo: So, in February 2023 Synod voted for same-sex blessings, but the conservatives cried foul: there should have been a more rigorous vote, they said – a two-thirds majority in each house of Synod – because this was a matter affecting doctrinal change. It seemed to me that they had a point – the reformers were being a bit dishonest when they dismissed this – because in reality this reform probably was opening the door to same-sex marriage, wasn't it?

John: I don't want to get too immersed in the politics of General Synod here, but whether allowing prayers for those in a same-sex marriage is to change the doctrine of marriage, something that Synod had previously undertaken not to do at this stage, is questionable – as is the question of whether teaching on marriage is a doctrine. If Synod were to vote for allowing same-sex marriage in church, as I hope it will one day, it would most certainly be a change in teaching on marriage. For the present, the Church of England is in a very new situation: that it has a different understanding of marriage from society.

Theo: It seemed to me that the delicate politics of the LLF process made honest reflection on all this impossible. We needed the archbishops, or at least one of them, to set out a positive vision, to admit that the Church's teaching on sex and marriage was changing. But they had to pretend that the Church was sticking with the old teaching – no sex outside straight marriage.

John: There is much on which to reflect: from where I stand, there are at least two separate but interlinking issues. The Church of England is probably not yet ready to introduce same-sex marriage in church, but if we are to be supportive and affirming of gay people we have to accept that sex for them will have to take place without a marriage in church and they should not be condemned for it. That is why some of us began to talk about relationships that are monogamous and faithful: the proper test of whether sex in a relationship is to be affirmed or not, it seems to me. We need, therefore, two new teachings: one on sex and one on marriage. We need to argue for a change in teaching on

INTRODUCTION

marriage and, until that change happens, no longer put a blanket condemnation on sex outside marriage. As long as we do, we seem to be suggesting that a committed monogamous relationship, whether homosexual or heterosexual, is on a par with a promiscuous lifestyle. There is also the question, which might not seem significant to many outside the Church, of whether clergy should be allowed to enter into same-sex secular marriage. I think it would be odd for clergy not to be permitted to enter into relationships that they are able to affirm in their ministry.

Theo: Yes, as well as introducing same-sex blessings, the LLF process is also meant to be issuing new guidance on gay clergy, and whether they can be in sexual relationships. The current rules, from 1991, say they can't. Obviously this is also something the Church is failing to move forward on.

John: It is indeed. An apology was issued by the Church of England to LGBT+ people about the way in which they had been treated in the past – but still very little has altered since 1991. The frustration of gay people is entirely understandable. It is time for change!

Theo: Maybe we can conclude by noting that last autumn, just as we were beginning to collect the chapters in this book, there was a significant development. Justin Welby, having been carefully quiet about his own position, got off the fence when talking to *The Rest is Politics* podcast. He said that stability and fidelity are what matter in relationships, straight or gay (which was more or less Jeffrey John's line a few decades earlier). He said it in a casual way, as if he'd thought it for years, but in reality it was the first time that he'd clearly moved away from the official teaching. I think this shows that the Church's leadership has shifted in a reformist direction, but doesn't yet know how to articulate it. It fears that speaking about it will split the Church. But reformist leadership is needed, or we'll have years of more muddle. And the conservatives will seem more theologically coherent than the reformers, who currently seem a bit disingenuous, inching forward an agenda that they don't dare spell out, or just going with the flow.

John: And then Welby resigned! It seems to me imperative that change comes about soon. The present situation is an insult to gay people and a missional disaster: most young people see the Church's stance on sexuality as offensive. We hope and pray that this collection of views will help in moving things forward.

We ought to conclude by making our own apology to all gay people: it might be difficult for them to read the above pontificating by two straight men. Our only defence is that we yearn to see them celebrated as equal and invaluable members of the body of Christ made in God's image, and no longer as a 'problem' to be solved. We hope and pray that this collection of essays will help to enable just that.

Notes

1 https://www.churchofengland.org/resources/living-love-and-faith (accessed 24.03.25).

2 https://www.cofe-worcester.org.uk/living-in-love-and-faith--a-letter-from-our-bishops.php (accessed 24.03.25).

3 https://www.oxford.anglican.org/news/same-sex-marriage-in-cofe.php (accessed 24.03.25).

4 https://www.cofe-worcester.org.uk/an-open-letter-from-bishop-john.php (accessed 24.03.25).

PART I

Bible

I

Beyond Patriarchy: Scripture and Tradition

MIRANDA THRELFALL-HOLMES

Not everything in the Bible is holy

'If your friend told you to jump off a cliff, would you?'

Most of us can remember being asked this, in exasperated tones, by a parental figure in our lives. It's a question the Bible asks of us in the dialogue between Jesus and the tempter (Matt. 4.1–11, Luke 4.1–13, with a much shorter reference in Mark 1.12–13). Having been foiled in his first attempts by Jesus' knowledge of and confidence in Scripture, the tempter turns to Scripture itself as a tool of temptation.

We're used to hearing that the devil twists Scripture, so what I find fascinating in this exchange is that the tempter quotes Scripture accurately. In reply, Jesus doesn't dispute that the quotation is accurate: he simply quotes another verse. In doing so, Jesus – and the compiler of Luke's Gospel – give us a mini masterclass in the use and abuse of Scripture. It is perfectly valid, as Jesus models for us here, to agree that yes, Scripture does say X – but it also says Y, and on balance that seems more helpfully applicable to the particular issue, situation or temptation that we are currently faced with.

I start with this hermeneutical principle because it is a highly important one when it comes to considering how we might look towards a new teaching on sex and marriage. I have no intention, in this brief chapter, of rehearsing again the arguments for and against conservative or progressive interpretations of each of the well-known 'clobber texts' on sex, sexuality and gender. Anyone who is interested in this topic will either have already made up their mind on the interpretation of those texts, or can readily find in-depth analyses from a variety of perspectives elsewhere.

Here, I want to suggest much more simply that, yes, much of the Bible does indeed assume a hetero-normative, patriarchal worldview. It's a worldview in which sex is considered primarily in terms of procreation; women are considered primarily in terms of their relationship to men; and men are valued primarily in terms of how well they measure up to a particular standard of masculinity. However, just because much of the Bible was written within a context where those assumptions went largely unnoticed and unquestioned, it does not mean that following the Bible faithfully today means imbibing the socio-cultural norms of the ancient Near East. To paraphrase what Jesus said to the tempter – yes, you're right, Scripture does indeed say that. But it also says many other things, which are far more healthy and life-giving, and will lead us to sensible, rather than destructive, behaviour.

This is foundational to understanding the way in which our complex historic inheritance of teaching about sex and marriage has developed. One of the criticisms often levied at those of us who dare suggest that a new teaching on sex and marriage might be healthier is that we are simply 'succumbing to the spirit of the age'. We all do well to examine closely what is really motivating and inspiring us. But as a 'gotcha', where this criticism falls down is in its denial of the historical reality that our biblical texts themselves are all, inevitably, suffused with the spirit of successive ages. Our faith is incarnational. In being 'fleshed out' in dialogue with successive specific contexts and cultures, God's w/Word has inevitably been shaped in part by each, as well as deeply challenging each.

Women were seen in much of the ancient world, philosophically speaking, as faulty men. They were also seen reproductively, in a context that had only a limited understanding of reproductive science, as not much more than simply receptive 'land' into which male seed was planted to grow.

Women were, as a result, seen essentially as property. Let's be honest about the fact that much of what is seen as a 'traditional sexual ethic' is in reality about controlling access to women as property; about respecting the property rights of men in respect of 'their' women; and about controlling paternity, and thus family lines and inheritance patterns. In the Ten Commandments, sex is primarily referenced in property terms rather than as an act in its own right. Coveting your neighbour's wife – that is, wishing to take her from him for yourself – is described as sinful in exactly the same terms as coveting his farm animals (ox or ass) or real estate (house).

But women are not property. We are beautifully and wonderfully made, in the image of God. We are not inferior to men, nor the possessions of men. So anything biblical that relates to, or derives from, an archaic and damaging view that sees us as such is to be jettisoned. I'd be tempted to say 'is to be disregarded' – but we need in fact to pay deep regard to such views, given the damage they have caused and continue to cause to so many, and very explicitly and consciously reject them.

Changing Church teaching on sex

The way the Church has thought and taught about sex and marriage has changed radically over time. A stark example comes from the Lambeth Conferences of the early twentieth century. In 1920, the report of the Lambeth Conference condemned 'the teaching, which, under the name of science and religion, encourages married people in the deliberate cultivation of sexual union as an end in itself'. The bishops explained that their view was not simply about emphasizing the importance of procreation but also to emphasize 'the paramount importance in married life of deliberate and thoughtful self-control'.

Just ten years later, the report of the 1930 Lambeth Conference took an entirely different line. Now, the conference confidently 'declares that the functions of sex as a God-given factor in human life are essentially noble and creative'. In 1930 even the bishops –

in stark contrast to the 1888 report which was too terrified even to define 'impurity' lest they corrupt the young – advocated for good sex education: 'before the child's emotional reaction to sex is awakened, definite information should be given in an atmosphere of simplicity and beauty'.

This historical example of a change in teaching is so sharp as to be at risk of giving us theological whiplash. It clearly alerts us to the fact that it is simply not true to say that the Church has always had one consistent teaching on these intimate matters. Nor is it true to say, as we often hear in the contemporary debates about same-sex relationships, that the Church has consistently viewed sex within heterosexual marriage as a good and holy thing. It would be more true to say that for quite a lot of Christian history, sex, including sex within heterosexual marriage, has been viewed as a rather regrettable necessity of the human condition, and a rather unpleasant reminder of the animal aspect of humanity. Marriage has been viewed not as an ideal, but as a damage-limitation exercise within which to contain and constrain the human libido.

It is also true to say that the Church's teachings on sex and marriage have been both gendered, heavily influenced by patriarchal assumptions about gender roles; and class-bound, with very different teachings, expectations and praxis around marriage for different classes of society. Both of these elements, neither of which stem inherently from the Church itself but from the society(ies) in which the Church has been incarnate over time, have themselves inevitably changed and shifted over the Church's 2,000 years of existence.

All of which is to say that I reject arguments to maintain 'conservative' teachings on the basis that they are what the Church has always taught. This is simply not true. But to the extent that it is true that for much of the Church's history sex has been viewed with suspicion, that is a teaching that I believe it would be healthy and life-giving for us to explicitly change. The view of the 1930 Lambeth Conference, that 'the functions of sex as a God-given factor in human life are essentially noble and creative', seems like a good place to start.

A feminist perspective: good sex and bad sex

Much of what has been written and taught about sex has, inevitably given the patriarchal context of the last few thousand years, been conceptualized from a male perspective. This has most obviously shaped concerns around paternity and associated questions of inheritance. Women know that the children they have given birth to are theirs, while men have to take it on trust. This has shaped teaching and practice around marriage to the extent that it has been about controlling male access to women, giving rise to the well-known history of gendered double standards around sexual activity.

Perhaps less obviously, the ways in which sexual activity has been conceptualized has also been shaped more by male than by female experience. Because we tend to be rather coy about what we're actually talking about when we talk about sex, this can easily go unnoticed and thus unchallenged. To be explicit, the embodied experience of sex – good sex – as a woman is different to that of a man. For men, good sex is generally conceptualized as what one might call a 'one shot' experience, culminating in the production of semen in orgasm. For women with a clitoris, good sex can be experienced in a considerably more open-ended way. Orgasm can follow orgasm, each delightfully different. No act of insemination needs to occur for a woman to find sex ultimately satisfying.

For both men and women, the experience of good sex is one of pleasure and delight: but I suggest that the extent to which sex has been viewed primarily in productive and penetrative terms, rather than in terms of open-ended delight, is a side-effect of the patriarchal lens.

The same might also be true if we consider what bad sex looks like. Men using sex as an act of violence is sadly all too common. Rape (of both women and men) is widely used not only as an individual act of intimidation and violence but also, on an industrial scale, in conflicts all over the world, as a weapon of war and genocide. If theologically reflective men have been aware of this propensity – at the worst, to use sex as a violent weapon of oppression rather than an expression of mutual delight – no wonder that a male-dominated theology of sex has viewed it as something that needs to be controlled. The idea that marriage to a woman will help domesticate otherwise wild men has been a consistent thread in much teaching on marriage.

From a feminist perspective, this puts a hugely unfair burden on women. While it is of course possible for men to be sexually abused by women, bad sex is overwhelmingly experienced by women as the abused rather than the abuser. Given many women's experiences of rape, sexual abuse and coercive control within marriage – and, indeed, of marriage itself being a societal tool by which women's agency and rights have been diminished – marriage as a putative solution to the problem of male sexual violence looks very different. Any teaching that valorizes heterosexual marriage as the answer to male sexual violence or male sexual energy is both unfair and inadequate. Women deserve a teaching that valorizes their own sexual energy and pleasure as much as men's; a teaching that can distinguish between good sex and bad sex and teach adolescents how to recognize the difference; and a teaching that actively corrects the historic and current abuse of women, children and adolescents in the name of patriarchy.

Scripture

One deeply regrettable consequence of a conservative reaction to increasingly liberal societal attitudes around homosexuality has been to undermine the progress that has been made in seeing women and men as fundamentally equal. Arguments that view the ideal of marriage as being between a man and a woman have to justify why this is the case, and therefore such arguments tend to rest ultimately on archaic understandings of women as 'complementary' – that is, fundamentally different to men, and ultimately inherently inferior to them. To the extent that these are theological arguments, they have unfortunately brought back into contemporary discourse both a deeply flawed understanding of men as more closely approximating the divine than women, and a deeply flawed literalist approach to Scripture.

So we find ourselves needing to reach back for feminist points about gender equality before God that were made decades ago, or in some cases, centuries ago. These are not primarily points about sexual or homosexual activity, but challenge the fundamental premise that male and female are two different categories of human, whom God relates to in different ways. In this brief chapter there is not room to rehearse all of these, but perhaps the most obvious is Galatians 3.27–28 – a text so radical that the Church has not yet, in its 2,000-year history, found itself able or willing to fully embrace it: 'As many of you as were baptized into Christ have clothed yourselves with Christ. There is no longer Jew or Greek, there is no longer slave or free, there is no longer male and female; for all of you are one in Christ Jesus.' At a stroke, race, nationality, economic status, social class, political status and gender roles are all set aside as being – at most – secondary considerations for the Church.

Obviously, it was not historical fact then or now that these distinctions were physically or socially erased. But it does seem to me that our emerging teaching on sex and marriage must take seriously the idea that these markers of identity – whether biologically or socially constructed – are no longer, in Christ, of theological significance. There is no first-, second- and third-class seating in the kingdom of God. Men had been very significantly valorized as closer to God in much of the thought of the time, whether Jewish or Greek – but now, we are told, that distinction no longer applies. The same applies to race, nationality and so on. None of these social markers of identity have any relative value once we are baptized: we are all, then, equally children of God. The use of 'children' as a metaphor in verse 26 is surely deliberate – male and female children had a very different status historically, but here such distinctions are being very consciously set aside. All are valued equally as co-heirs.

Our teaching on Christian marriage, therefore, must be based on it being a relationship of equals, of two beloved co-heirs of God choosing to go through life together for mutual support and companionship. We must explicitly reject any lingering taint of historic views of men as superior to women.

Another key text for thinking theologically about sex is the Song of Songs. This is an astonishing book within Scripture, filled with images of delight in a lover's body and physicality, and of the mutual joy of desiring and being desired. It's also remarkable for taking the form of a dialogue, almost a playscript, in which women's voices are heard in their own terms. Song of Songs offers a dramatically different view of sex from that usually associated with the pages of the Bible. Here, sex is not portrayed primarily in terms of penetration, or procreation; nor is it set within an explicitly marital framework. Here, sex is celebrated as a multi-sensory delight. It is about touch, scent, sound; about arousal, frustrated and satisfied desire, and delighting in every aspect of the beloved's body. As a text for what good sex could look like it is hard to beat. A new scriptural teaching on sex and marriage should take Song of Songs with the utmost seriousness, as a piece of Scripture that embodies something of how mutual sexual passion and desire are elements of our God-given embodied createdness.

The most extensive reflection on sex, sexual morality and marriage in the Bible comes in 1 Corinthians. Chapter 5 points out what seems to have been a particularly notorious example of sexual immorality among the Corinthian church members, of a man having sex with his own father's wife. Paul points out, in this context, that when he told the church to 'shun sexual immorality' he wasn't advocating separating themselves from a different class of sexually immoral people, but challenging the church members themselves to be aware of their own behaviour. It's an important warning against the temptation to divide the world into 'goodies' and 'baddies', and to assume that insiders can't behave badly – something that lies behind a lot of domestic and church-based abuse.

A new teaching on sex and marriage needs to take very seriously indeed all that we have learned in recent decades about the dynamics of abuse.

In Chapter 6, Paul generalizes more broadly about sexual

activity and marriage. His teaching here is interestingly pragmatic rather than dogmatic. At the heart of 1 Corinthians 6, and key to Paul's teaching here, is the arresting central image of the body as a temple. As people who have been baptized and who partake in Holy Communion, our bodies are part of Christ, and temples of the Holy Spirit – so what we do with them matters. Paul has often been seen as being rather negative about the body, but this is in fact a very body-positive approach.

So finally – if our bodies are temples, what does Scripture tell us about temples, and how might this inform a refreshed teaching? They are not to be the scenes of money-making transactions (Mark 11.15–17). They are to be approached with delight and joy (Ps. 122). They are to be revered as places where one meets with God in a very specific way (1 Kings 8), though God is not limited to them or by them (Acts 17). They are essentially ephemeral (Luke 21).

A new teaching on sex must take our bodies seriously, as places – which come in all shapes and sizes – of delight and wonder. Places to enjoy and explore with reverence and respect. Places in which we encounter God and one another, in all our literal and metaphorical nakedness.

2

Holy Wedlock and Intimate God: A Biblical Teaching of Marriage

BARNABAS PALFREY

This chapter is on Christian biblical teaching about marriage and sex.

We can too easily overlook the intensity of the biblical holding together of *individuality and relationality* with *communality and collectivity*. We Christians, certainly, cannot with integrity separate our sexual lives from our contemplations of the body of Christ or our anticipatory entries into the eschatological community known as the kingdom of God. And yet we each ought also to heed Rowan Williams's observation that our frantic attempts at getting sex 'right' are 'doomed'.[1] Realizing this is a first negative step in any decent spirituality of sex.

My argument has three stages. First, that however mundanely sensible the institution of marriage may be, Christian marriage is more an eschatological sacrament of salvation than a mundane ordinance of Creation.

Second, I will argue that questions around sex and marriage today lead to a more general 'fork in the road' for Christian thinking about God. Granted that divine grace finally sows meaning and cosmos rather than chaos and confusion, Christians must decide whether their Creator is therefore a General Franco in the Sky, whose worship ruthlessly enforces some more-or-less known, finite hierarchy and ordering of things. Or, alternatively, is God instead the Infinite Sponsor of order and meaning coming to us, ever graciously, in the manifold plurality of the world? This radical choice concerns not just sexual matters but also many varied questions of disability, culture, race, religion and much else besides.

Third, I will argue that Eugene Rogers makes a powerfully apposite move when he defines marriage as an ascetic practice.[2] The Greek word *ascesis* means 'discipline' or 'exercise', a practice beloved of all the major philosophical traditions of the Roman period. In its monastic development, informed by centuries of martyrdom and digestions of Platonism, Christian asceticism took on a more aggressively austere aspect of subjugation of the body, but whatever the alien oddities and pitfalls modern eyes may perceive in this tradition, we Christians would nevertheless be foolish simply to distance ourselves from our powerful and ambiguous heritage here. A doctrine of marriage as an ascetic practice articulates a riposte to Christians who can imagine the positive spiritual sense of sex and marriage only on the basis of sex-gender complementarity or the production of children.

These three stages of argument now need filling out and justifying with more detailed contents.

1 A sacrament of salvation, not a static ordinance of Creation

In the Hebrew Scriptures, God's marriage to Israel abounds as a figure of the Covenant, God's faithful delight and sorrow frequently contrasted with Israel's faithlessness. Rowan Williams has observed that nowhere is this theme more striking than in the book of the prophet Hosea, whose tragic marriage to a prostitute enacts a parable of God's own 'exposure to humiliation ... at the mercy of the perceptions of an uncontrollable partner'.[3]

If anything, this motif of divine-human marriage gets raised to an even higher pitch in the Christian New Testament. In the Gospels, Jesus teaches faithfulness to the matrimonial bond imagined in Eden (even if his disciples seem to have left wives to follow him, at least temporarily), while he frequently employs the image of a wedding feast for the kingdom of God. St Paul, meanwhile, conceives bodily sexual union extremely realistically in its significance for individuals' salvation; and the wider Pauline Letter to the Ephesians contains a justly famous proposal that human marriage figures the mystery of Christ-and-the-Church (and vice versa). And in Revelation, John the Seer beholds the marriage of the Church-Bride with Jesus, her triumphant Bridegroom.

These biblical marriage images have been supplemented in Christian history by reception of the Hebrew Song of Songs. For 1,500 years until modernity, the Song shared the prize with Genesis and the Psalms for the most Christian-commented portions of the Old Testament. The Song's frequently breathless eroticism taught generations of monastics, in particular, to know and sense the passionate asymmetrical love-relationship between Christ and the Church, and Christ and each individual soul as the Bride of Christ.

Note, too, how the Gospel of John already seems to reference the Song in its unforgettable story of the lone Mary Magdalene in the garden of the resurrection, as her yearning heartbreak gives way in stages to astounded joy, intimacy and then restraint. Only John records a garden near the place of Jesus' crucifixion, and his being temporarily laid there in a virgin tomb (womb?) on the Friday afternoon, along with half his body weight in myrrh and aloes. 'I come to my garden, my sister, my bride. I gather my myrrh with my spice' (Song 5.1); 'My beloved has gone down to his garden, to the beds of spices' (Song 6.2).

I think the very prominence of these biblical meditations suggests a first reason why Christians should seek their scriptural account of marriage *here* rather more than in 'safer'-seeming biblical snippets about mundane moral and social order. It makes little biblical or doctrinal sense to hold apart mundane creation and salvation in Christ. And, it is also clear which of these two is the senior partner. As Rogers writes, 'earthly realities do not define heavenly realities, even if we learn earthly things first': instead, 'heavenly realities redefine earthly ones'.[4]

A second reason for approaching marriage by this biblical route is that Christians anyway need to face up to this ubiquitous biblical image of divine-human marriage, in all its seeming inscription of normative heterosexuality and an almighty (if also vulnerable) husband. As the radical post-Christian feminist Mary Daly famously objected, 'if God is male then the male is God': a conclusion as ruinous as the oppression of sexual minorities. But as we will explore shortly, it turns out that if Christians could only 'lean in' *not only* to the better elements in the Bible's more mundane commendations of marriage *but even more* to its outlandishly offensive talk of God as heavenly husband to the wifely creation, then the divine marital reference will proceed to 'queer' itself and its stable-seeming references to mundane gender and sex. And all this while enabling ongoing discriminations of sense, reason and institution.

A third and final reason, as Rogers also points out, is that this last effect is intimated already in St Paul's famous declaration in his Letter to the Galatians that in Christ 'there is no longer Jew or Greek, there is no longer slave or free, there is no longer male and female' (Gal. 3.28). Rogers unpacks Paul's careful formulation here:

> Paul is quoting Genesis about 'male and female'. He negates not the parties, but the pair. In Christ – to put the negation in modern terms – there is no compulsory heterosexuality. The human goal is not complementarity but Christ.[5]

In sum, the claim here is that the horizons of life in Christ bar us from reading a moral theology of sex-gender complementarity into the biblical Creation stories. A Christological and eschatological horizon for mundane marriage, on the one hand, along with, reciprocally, a figuratively marital horizon for Christ and the kingdom of God on the other, irresistibly set about unpicking the patriarchy and hetero-normativity.

2 Neither an almighty husband nor a Heavenly General Franco

In Chapter 5 of the Letter to the Ephesians, the scriptural matter of human marriage and divine salvation achieves crescendo. The writer begins by instructing his readers all to 'be subject to one another out of reverence for Christ'. But then, even so, he proceeds upon patriarchally differentiated instructions for husbands and wives (Eph. 5.22ff.). Wives are told to 'be subject to your husbands as you are to the Lord' (Eph. 5.22), because 'the husband is the head of the wife just as Christ is the head of the church, the body of which he is the Saviour' (Eph. 5.23). Then husbands are told to 'love your wives, just as Christ loved the church and gave himself up for her ... cleansing her with the washing of water by the word ... so that she may be holy and without blemish' (Eph. 5.25–27): 'husbands should love their wives as they do their own bodies' (Eph. 5.28). And then, in a stunning interpretative move, the writer proposes that it is *the situation of Christ and the Church* that is the true 'reason a man will leave his father and mother and be joined to his wife, and the two will become one flesh' (Eph. 5.31; quoting Gen. 2.24). Then he puts it the other way round: human marriage and sexual differentiation 'is a great mystery, and I am applying it to Christ and the church' (Eph. 5.32).

Christ is here gendered male and the Church as female, according to a clear patriarchal asymmetry. But Rogers notes that the Church has always been made up of men as well as women, while for most of its history an all-male priesthood has represented the Church as male. As he concludes: 'A man as well as a woman can represent the church.'[6] And no less pertinent for the practical reception of this passage is the manner in which the risen Christ has come to include every permutation of sex and gender. The male body of Christ is also female as his bride and as the Marian Church, even as Jesus interpreted as the divine Word is also beyond and the very source of gender. By the early third century, Clement of Alexandria (d. c. 215) could picture Christ suckling believers with milk from his breasts, an image taken up anew by twelfth-century Cistercian monks, who also imagined crawling up into the wound in Christ's side as into his womb, from where to be reborn.[7]

In a version of what, in fact, Israel *already* meant – the excess, pluriformity and conceptual non-containability that an Incarnate God underlines – comes here explicitly to encompass the whole community of the redeemed with their Lord in a dynamic correspondence of mundane and heavenly. The back-and-forth between earthly marriage and heavenly salvation spins apart the ostensive stability of its gendered equations. In the light of *Christ* – his body, 'marriage' and community – lesbian and gay people, or transgendered people, or gender-ambiguous people, or people born with biologically indeterminate sex, must no longer be subordinated to sexual regimes that exclude and marginalize them.

Behind the proof-texting that unwittingly disrespects Scripture by treating it as un-plural, lumpen and magically pure, I suggest there can often lie a vicious anxiousness to exhibit the world as one *divinely finite* moral order. Venerable scriptures get pressed into the service of crass intuitions about a physical-spiritual cosmos, along with frankly incredible assertions about divine spiritual and moral intentions supposedly exhibited on the surfaces of our evolutionarily emergent bodies. Christianity reduces to a kind of old-time theme-park in which plastic simulacra of what once passed for serious thinking 'live' on in zombie-land.

Furthermore, in treating God as akin to some inferable consciousness or intentionality (like ours, only disembodied and bigger), encoded within the bare facts of the world no more cryptically than a crossword clue, the 'conservative' position may then easily be led to the monstrosity of God – or our dear Jesus – as, in effect, a Heavenly General Franco. The identity of the god is collapsed into the presumed authority of some finite hierarchy and order: a single known or knowable 'cosmos' into which all difference must be forcibly fitted, whether as more-or-less esteemed or more-or-less excluded. There is something about collective religion and individual spiritual vision that can breed this kind of evil fantasy.

Some may worry, though, that in the scenario for sex and marriage that I am sketching here, bodies may have ceased to mean anything in some rush towards disembodied subjectivity. Yet instead, as Rogers insists, '[a] Christological account of gender gives bodies more, not fewer, ways to matter':

> Because the body of the medieval Christ both retains his circumcision and gains a womb, Christ resembles an intersex person. Because the body of Christ is male in the history of Jesus and female in the history of the church, Christ resembles a transsexual person. Because Christ can be the bridegroom to a male believer, he resembles the same sex spouse. Gender does not limit Christ, because he is its Lord.[8]

On the more mundane side of things, it is also surely nonsense to imagine that individual body parts and correlate body-wholes each mean simply *the same things* across all their examples and occasions, or else nothing at all. My own penis on my living socialized body, for example, will always mean *something*, but it never means precisely the same thing each time. Furthermore, the mistake in demanding that kinds of bodies and kinds of body-parts mean particular things immediately and universally lies in a 'cosmologizing' *disembodiment from factual society*. Bodies mean within the complexities of society, not within fantasized pure cosmic horizons. My penis might perhaps do some rather similar things were I married instead to a man, but undoubtedly it would then carry some interestingly distinct social meanings; just as likewise were I identifying socially as a transwoman. Embodied meaning does not vanish to nothing simply because it is recognized to be plural, social and political, as well as existential. Only an approach that imagines the human individual as disembodied from society demands that human bodies conform to metaphysical horizons established by their forms simply as living objects.

The question becomes therefore whether it is indeed possible to honour God as the Infinite Sponsor of human sexual and other plurality, without thereby dissolving away meaning, social order and discrimination of holiness. *Is* there a gracious and meaningful theological alternative to the all-too-finite and all-too-effective idolatry of General Franco in the Sky?

3 Marriage as the ascetic practice of the body's grace

I have no biological children of my own (I greatly cherish my wife's two grandchildren), yet I feel immensely privileged to have benefited in my own childhood from the dedicated and difficult way of marriage. I also see all around me fruits formed and being formed via this institution, which despite its many ambiguities and easy horrors acts as a bulwark against childhoods spent enduring the adolescent self-indulgences of adults. I also think of older gay friends now able to retire together in the safety of legal, financial and social-cultural recognition only recently extended to them. All this I find true, and yet a Christian spirituality of sex and marriage requires more.

For a long time, Christian history has exalted spiritual desire – spiritual and divine *eros* as a co-truth of spiritual and divine *agape* – while failing to be positive about sexual desire contemplated and enacted between human lovers. And yet, we Christians will not find it straightforward to unpick this historical Christian hesitancy without falling headlong into contrasting spiritual mistakes of misplaced sensuality or worldliness. Certainly, Christians will not be helped by naïvely enthusiastic affirmations of the spiritual positivity of sex. (It would be more realistic to follow the linking of sex, agony and death in the post-Catholic pornographer and sexual transgressive, Georges Bataille.)

In a classic essay, 'The Body's Grace', originally given as an address to the 1989 conference of the UK Lesbian and Gay Christian Movement, Rowan Williams suggests some bearings for a Christian spirituality of sex. He identifies the body's grace in sex with one's body becoming perceived for another's delight such that we become 'given over to the creation of joy in another'.[9] This 'being formed in our humanity by the loving desire of another'[10] is the opposite of the graceless perversion that is sex 'without risk'

– that is, 'without the dangerous knowledge that my joy depends upon someone else's, as theirs does on mine'.[11] Williams suggests that Christians will be the better equipped to identify gracious sexual experience the more they are also starting to understand themselves entirely as 'the object of the causeless, loving delight of God ... the object of God's love for God through incorporation into the community of God's Spirit and the taking-on of the identity of God's child'. In other words, sex is one signal and fraught arena for learning entry into grace.

In all this, *same-sex* love possesses a peculiar gift for Christians, Williams suggests, in posing baldly to us the question of the meaning of sexual desire 'in itself, not considered [as] instrumental to some other process, such as the peopling of the world'.[12] Williams finds sex theologically and spiritually relevant in its 'nonfunctional joy': that is, in its joy 'whose material "production" is an embodied person aware of grace'.

To this spirituality of *the body's grace* in sex I propose we add Rogers's more recent account of the *ascetic practice* of marriage. Reminiscent of Williams, Rogers writes of how 'my destiny lies in Another whom I cannot control' and how this makes sexuality and marriage into 'practice for life with God'.[13] This 'preparation' that marriage proposes is 'an ascetic enterprise' in the classic sense of 'a spiritual discipline or training whereby lesser goods serve greater ones'. Rogers cites Russian tradition that the marriage vows derive from monastic ones – 'chastity ("forsaking all others"), poverty ("for richer for poorer", "with all my worldly goods I thee endow"), and stability ("till death do us part")' – and that the marriage crowns received at Eastern Orthodox weddings symbolize crowns of martyrdom.[14] Marriage is therefore not about 'self-satisfaction' but is instead 'a mechanism for turning longing into charity', *eros* into *agape*.[15]

Rogers's contribution appropriates the language of monastic spirituality to paint the practice of marriage squarely on the historical canvas of Christian spiritual yearning. Where Williams insists that sexual faithfulness makes space for the grace of sex to abound by granting the partners time for mutual recognition, amid a 'commitment not to run away from the perception of the other',[16] Rogers tells us how, in transfiguring *amor* as *caritas*, the promises and graces of marriage are akin to those of baptism and every Christian ascetic witness to the kingdom of God.

Conclusion: because I am individual and collective

Anglicans ought to regard marriage as an icon and sacrament of Christ's salvation, and not reduce it to an ordinance of created nature alone. For the sake of Jesus, they must complicate every imagination of an Almighty Husband and fight down with all their strength the evil fascinations of a Heavenly General Franco. There should be gay marriage in church. May we each, as we are called, find ways to attend to our body's grace in ascetic witness and sharing of joy. All this is biblical, and it is to be fought for: just as the Church once fought the mistaken traditionalism of Arius and then the pinched rationalism of Nestorius (each of whom had their scriptural proof-texts).

Karl Rahner somewhere characterizes marriage as the smallest church. This only emphasizes how sex can never be simply a private thing for Christians. And yet, the wintry conditions of our historical realities frequently ameliorate the impossible-seeming Christian hope for spiritual individuality in divine collectivity. For example, lesbian and gay Anglican clergy, wrongly denied access to marriage, may well entertain spiritual-theological regard for the institution while yet entering into less regular living arrangements, without contradiction. And although straight sex and cohabitation outside marriage don't yet exhibit the entire communal-collective 'thing', still, in some circumstances at least, they may gesture an icon of Christ rather better than grimly awkward refusals.

Undoubtedly there is cost to belonging in a church, a marriage, or a marriage-like relationship – in a community, as a collective, to an institution – if only in aggravation. These words from the great married lay Roman Catholic spiritual writer and thinker Friedrich von Hügel (1852–1925) seem pertinent to all our spiritual belongings:

There is no such thing as appurtenance to a particular religious body without cost – cost to the poorer side of human nature and cost even, in some degree and way, to the better side of that same nature. Hence the need of an increasingly wise discrimination – of a generous payment of the cost where it affects the poorer side, and of a careful limitation of the cost, and a resourceful discovery of compensation elsewhere, where the cost affects the better side of our nature.[17]

May we all learn to pay the cost generously and also limit the cost carefully, with wise discrimination. For as with all our other callings, our individual sexual-marital histories can only emerge from the holy smokes of joy, pain, awe and vulnerability that fill the temples of our bodies.

Notes

1 Rowan Williams, 'The body's grace', in Eugene F. Rogers, *Theology and Sexuality: Classic and Contemporary Readings*, Oxford: Blackwell (2002), pp. 309–21, 310.
2 See Eugene F. Rogers, 'Same-sex marriage as an ascetic practice in the light of Romans 1 and Ephesians 5', *Modern Believing*, 55.2 (2014), pp. 115–25.
3 Williams, 'The body's grace', pp. 309–21, 319.
4 Rogers, 'Same-sex marriage', p. xx.
5 Rogers, 'Same-sex marriage', p. xx.
6 Rogers, 'Same-sex marriage', p. xx.
7 Rogers, 'Same-sex marriage', p. xx.
8 Eugene F. Rogers, 'Same-sex complementarity: a theology of marriage', *Christian Century*, 17 May 2011, pp. 26–31, 31.
9 Williams, 'The body's grace', p. 313.
10 Williams, 'The body's grace', p. 317.
11 Williams, 'The body's grace', p. 314.
12 Williams, 'The body's grace', p. 318.
13 Rogers, 'Same-sex marriage', p. xx.
14 Rogers, 'Same-sex marriage', p. xx.
15 Rogers, 'Same-sex marriage', p. xx.
16 Williams, 'The body's grace', p. 315.
17 Friedrich von Hügel, 1921, 'Responsibility in religious belief', in *Essays and Addresses on the Philosophy of Religion*, London and Toronto: J. M. Dent & Sons Ltd, pp. 3–19, 15.

PART 2

Church

3

Living Well with Difference: A Primer in Anglican Ecclesiology

STEVEN CROFT

The Church of England is amazing. After more than a century of secularization, by the grace of God we are able still to sustain a vibrant network of parish churches across every part of England, in continuity with patterns established many centuries ago. In every place there are priests, a congregation to provide welcome, prayer and worship offered, love and care extended to the wider community, and a witness given to the gospel. The Church of England has not withdrawn from inner urban communities and is still present in strength in the countryside. We have tens of thousands of clergy, licensed lay ministers, churchwardens and parish officers who give their time and dedicate their lives to the flourishing of these parish churches and communities. Thanks be to God.

As a Church we face many challenges – just like the Church did in every generation and every place. In our generation one of those challenges will be, undoubtedly, living with our very different views on human sexuality. But facing those challenges will require, of all of us, a deeper understanding of what it means to be the church and what it means to be the Church of England. Without this deeper understanding there is a real danger that some of the insights that undergird our very identity might be lost. This chapter explores that deeper understanding of what it means to be church and to be the Church of England.

A conversion experience

I've had several major conversion experiences through over 40 years of ordained ministry. One of the most memorable came in 1994. In my first decade in parish ministry, my deep conviction was that the parish church, the local church, meant everything. My second was that the heart of ministry and the only valid expression of ministry was evangelism: seeing men and women, children and young people come to faith.

This meant I invested just about all my energy in the growth of the local church in Halifax where I served as Vicar. I had very little time or awareness of the wider deanery or the diocese. I never served as a member of a Diocesan Synod until I became a diocesan bishop. Like many evangelical clergy of my generation, my ideas about the local church were shaped by a combination of the church growth movement, supplemented by the Vineyard and the powerful teaching ministry of John Wimber. The slogan coined by Bill Hybels, the once influential founding pastor of Willow Creek Church in Chicago, summed up my attitude: the local church is the hope of the world.

I still believe profoundly in the importance of evangelism and in the vital importance of the local church – but not as the fundamental expression of what it means to be the Church. My conversion – my deep change of mind – happened like this. In 1993 I was seconded to the team working on strategy for the Diocese of Wakefield. I began then to get a sense of what a diocese might be. The Diocesan Missioner, Stephen Cottrell, and I were sent away on a three-day conference in Windsor with a team from the diocese, to explore the good things that were happening elsewhere. The conference was led by David Ford, a theologian from Cambridge, and Robert Warren, newly appointed as National Officer for Evangelism.

I began the conference evaluating everything I heard through the twin lenses of the local congregation and evangelism. But as I listened to all that was being said, a dual realization dawned: first that God's mission was bigger than I had suspected and, second, that God's Church was much bigger than I had realized.

My eyes were opened in fresh ways to the scope of the mission of God: that God is active in the world to love the world; that God's purposes in mission are unfolding beyond the life of the Church; that God's vision is for the whole world to be renewed and remade; that the mission of God includes evangelism but is multidimensional and includes care for Creation; transforming unjust structures; reconciliation and loving service. These themes will almost certainly be familiar now as the themes of the Five Marks of Mission of the Anglican Communion.

It is not so much that the Church of God has a mission, as one theologian has said, but that the God of mission has a Church. As many others have said, mission for the Church is primarily about discovering what God is doing and seeking to join in.

And if God's mission is about the whole of our society and, indeed, the whole of God's world, then no local church, however large, can engage adequately with that mission. The parish where I served had a population of around 9,000 in a town with a population of over 120,000. We could not engage with many of the broader issues in that town. Our calling was simply to play our part in the whole.

I came to realize much later than I should have done that, for Anglicans, the basic unit of the Church is not the parish served by the priest but rather the diocese served and led by the bishop. This is no accident of history but a deep missional framing of our understanding. No local church can minister to the whole of a community. The diocesan structures we have inherited are shaped by, and serve, the mission of God.

The challenge of our differences on human sexuality

For the last decade, the Church of England has been seeking to discern how and whether to revise our response to gay and lesbian partnerships. In February 2023, the General Synod agreed to authorize new services, Prayers of Love and Faith, for use with those in stable, lifelong and faithful same-sex relationships. We agreed to revise our guidance for clergy in the conduct of their close relationships and are in the process of reconsidering whether clergy in same-sex marriages can be licensed by their bishop to new roles.

These measures seem very modest to many who would like the Church to go much further and solemnize same-sex marriage. However, to others these changes represent a departure from faithful biblical teaching, a watershed moment, a crossing of the Rubicon.

It is important to have a nuanced and accurate understanding of these differences. In 2022 I published an essay on my own change of mind on these questions, 'Together in Love and Faith'. Ever since, I have been in regular correspondence and conversation with a great many people on these issues across the Diocese of Oxford and beyond. My own perspective is that there is not a simple divide on these issues with some in favour of the changes and some against. There is instead a segmentation.

Overall, on my own reckoning and in the light of research, I would say around 60 per cent of clergy and congregations are in favour of change in a more inclusive direction; and there are at least four different groups in the remaining 40 per cent.

Some are *indifferent*: they are conservative in their views on sexuality but without strong feelings for or against the changes – and very much wanting the Church to address other and more pressing concerns. Some are genuinely *undecided* on what is from many perspectives a complex and challenging theological question. However, they are pulled towards a traditional view because of friends or communities who feel the issues more deeply.

Some hold a traditional view of marriage but are *accepting* that change is needed and very willing to work alongside and with others who take a more inclusive view to retain the maximum degree of fellowship, collaboration and unity. Pastoral reassurance is required for many in this group (including the assurance that no one need use Prayers of Love and Faith against their conscience). Finally, some hold a traditional view of marriage but are *resisting* any change, believing such a change to be a first-order issue of Christian doctrine and signalling a departure by the Church of England from the true faith.

There are no exact figures for the proportions of Anglican clergy and lay people who find themselves in each of the groups 2 to 5 (hence the dotted lines in the table below).

Those who want to use the prayers	Indifferent	Undecided/ concerned	Traditional Accepting	Traditional Resisting

Those in the traditional and accepting group seek both pastoral reassurance and some provision of particular ministries (for example, a bishop who shares their convictions to conduct confirmations in their parish). Those in the traditional but resisting group seek provision that goes much further and extends to a system of alternative legal, pastoral and spiritual oversight. The outworking of this alternative oversight would be a patchwork fragmentation of dioceses which (in my view) would do serious and permanent damage to the missional identity of the Church of England. These proposals and ideas therefore need to be examined very carefully through the lens of ecclesiology (what it means to be church) and missiology (what it means to engage in God's mission).

Understanding ecclesiology

In 2004 I was charged by Archbishop Rowan Williams with the task of setting up and leading a new national initiative, Fresh Expressions. The aim of Fresh Expressions was to take the ideas and concepts in a new report, *Mission-Shaped Church*, and help them to become normal across the Church of England and the Methodist Church. At the heart of *Mission-Shaped Church* was the desire to encourage the development of new Christian congregations through contextual mission, largely for those who were beyond the cultural reach of the existing Church.

I began to tour the country, visiting different dioceses. I imagined at the beginning that the major part of my work would be helping the Church to reflect on God's mission. In fact, overall I found a relatively strong and common sense of mission across the Church, summarized in the Five Marks of Mission. Instead, I found a massive deficit in careful thinking and reflection on what it means to be the Church, on ecclesiology. A typical Anglican preparing for ordained ministry or licensed lay ministry will have done several modules and assignments on mission. But the same person will have done almost no ecclesiology, no study of what it means to be church, either biblical or historical or contemporary. After all, we all know what it means to be church, surely?

My early experience of being a vicar shows that we do not. So does the experience of the Fresh Expressions movement: as soon as pioneers begin to develop church in new contexts and cultures, a whole range of new ecclesiological questions about the Church, ministry, sacraments, connection and governance begin to arise. Likewise, so does the experience of many a new incumbent today who finds himself or herself in a first parish with a radically different understanding of church and mission than the one in which they are formed.

My own reading focused in these years on ecclesiology. I discovered that there is no one kind of language about church but at least five different ways of exploring what church means:

1 Distilled ecclesiology – short summary statements describing the marks of the Church.
2 Descriptive ecclesiology – more extensive explorations of the wonder and mystery and reality of the Church.
3 Discerning and defining ecclesiology – developing guidelines for when a particular community is church, what needs to be present.
4 Derived ecclesiology – shaping principles that have a practical application for such things as church governance or ministry or practice.
5 Developmental ecclesiology that continually contrasts the reality of the Church with the ideal presented in Scripture and tradition.

In answering the questions about living well with difference, we need to go further than an answer to the question: what does it mean to be the Church? We are seeking to answer the question in a particular time and place and within a particular tradition. Therefore we also have to answer the question: what does it mean to be Anglican? And, specifically: what does it mean to be the Church of England?

Here it is helpful to turn to a set of values about the life of the Christian Church which, like the Five Marks of Mission, are rooted in the life of the Anglican Communion. Though these values are much older, they are less well known in the Church of England today.

In the nineteenth century the bishops of the Episcopal Church convened in Chicago to consider what it means to be the Anglican Church in dialogue with other Churches. The bishops passed a resolution citing four marks of Anglican identity. Their resolution was based on an 1870 essay by William Reed Huntingdon. Two years later, the third Lambeth Conference passed a similar resolution to determine four essential marks of the Anglican Communion:

1 The Holy Scriptures of the Old and New Testaments, as 'containing all things necessary to salvation', and as being the rule and ultimate standard of faith.
2 The Apostles' Creed, as the Baptismal Symbol; and the Nicene Creed, as the sufficient statement of the Christian faith.
3 The two Sacraments ordained by Christ Himself – Baptism and the Supper of the Lord – ministered with unfailing use of Christ's words of Institution, and of the elements ordained by Him.
4 The Historic Episcopate, locally adapted in the methods of its administration to the varying needs of the nations and peoples called of God into the Unity of His Church.

Although this 'quadrilateral' was framed as a vital tool in ecumenical dialogue, it has also formed something of a yardstick for measuring ecclesiological developments in Anglican church life: with both recognizing other provinces and recognizing fresh expressions of the Church and new congregations.

In an essay published almost 20 years ago, I attempted to develop the quadrilateral into a fundamental statement of Anglican identity for discerning the qualities needed in an Anglican fresh expression of the Church. The key development was – and remains – the addition of the Five Marks of Mission as a fifth arm, with the whole now revised and adapted here:

5 The comprehensive understanding of the Mission of God to the whole of creation and the whole of society as defined and described in the Anglican Communion's Five Marks of Mission.

These Five Marks of the Church are each fundamental to Anglican identity and the vision for what it means to be the Anglican Church. They preserve the creative space for different cultural expressions of the Church. They preserve the space and yet set boundaries for the different traditions within the Church of England and keep the relationships between these traditions within the framework of the historic episcopate. They provide, I would suggest, a yardstick for measuring how we live together with difference and what the boundaries of any pastoral reassurance and provision might be.

The provision of alternative ministry but not alternative oversight

So what does all of this mean for how we might live together well as Anglicans with differing convictions on same-sex relationships? Our Anglican understanding of the Church is that the fundamental unit of it is the diocese, not the parish. This understanding is based on our broad and deep understanding of the mission of God. It is entirely possible therefore to accommodate diversity of conviction between different parishes on these issues without serious disruption to Anglican integrity. It is entirely feasible to envisage alternate provision of episcopal ministry providing this is clearly defined. However, once this provision is conceived of, or becomes alternative oversight (with or without disruption), it begins seriously to disrupt our Anglican understanding of mission and what it means to be the church.

The Church of England holds to the view that all ministry is by the grace of God, that all ministers are imperfect, and that the grace of God in the sacraments is not invalidated by the imperfections or shortcomings – or the personal views – of individual ministers. For this reason I cannot in conscience hold to the view that provision of alternative episcopal ministry is theologically necessary on the grounds that a particular bishop supports – or has used – Prayers of Love and Faith.

However, I do continue to hold the view that in some circumstances the provision of alternative episcopal ministry may be expedient and helpful to some ministers and congregations in the context of the present difficult debates. We are constrained by our love for one another to seek the maximum degree of mutual support and help. In my view, this alternative provision of episcopal ministry extends to confirmations, to ordinations in certain circumstances, to ministerial reviews and to parish visits.

But to go beyond this to a structured form of permanent alternative oversight, to virtual dioceses and overlapping pastoral and legal jurisdictions, seems to me to erode significantly our understanding of the Church and of God's mission.

A Christ-like Church for the sake of God's world

The journey of conversion reached a new milestone as I came to the end of my ministry with Fresh Expressions, and prepared to take up the ministry of a bishop in the Diocese of Sheffield. In 2008 I was invited to give a talk to a Diocesan Conference about the future of the Church of England over the next generation. The invitation came with a rider: 'and we don't want your normal fresh expressions talk'.

I was compelled to ask the question: what is my vision for

the Church over the next decades? Perhaps you remain in a similar place. My own thinking made a significant turn at this point – mainly because I do not find (and have never found) the mechanics of mission or ecclesiology to be life-giving.

The key turn was to realize that underneath our understanding of both the Church and mission lies our understanding of Jesus Christ. In more technical language, our Christology needs to shape our missiology which needs to shape our ecclesiology. We are called as a Church to be like Jesus.

That fundamental insight undergirds the development of the vision statement for the Diocese of Sheffield and in the Diocese of Oxford where we seek to be a more Christ-like Church for the sake of God's world: more contemplative, compassionate and courageous (qualities drawn directly from the beatitudes of Matthew's Gospel). The same insight fed into my own theological contribution to the vision and strategy of the Church of England in 2020 which seeks to see: 'A Church for the whole nation which is Jesus Christ-centred and shaped by the Five Marks of Mission. A Church which is simpler, humbler, bolder.'

The same insight, I have to say, informed the longer, slower change of mind on the need for the Church to recognize and bless permanent, faithful, stable same-sex relationships. It is as we explore the priorities and character of Christ that hearts and minds on this issue are changed.

The Church of England is amazing because Jesus Christ is amazing. We should do all we can to preserve the unity of the Church in all our present diversity on human sexuality. But there are limits to what can be offered without undermining the very essence of our identity.

4

'In Christ'

JOHN INGE

> There is no longer Jew or Greek, there is no longer slave or free, there is no longer male and female; for all of you are one in Christ Jesus. (Gal. 3.28)

It is said that Anglican theology derives from attention to Scripture, tradition and the Church, the so-called 'three-legged stool' approach associated with Richard Hooker. I believe, rather, that a properly Anglican theology rests upon a more dynamic approach: Scripture, interpreted in the light of the living tradition of the Church, using reason and human experience. I shall argue here that this had profound implications as early as when St Paul was writing his letters, and it continues to do so now, not least for our understanding of sexual ethics.

I hear it observed that there is great dissension in the Church in our generation. True though that statement is, it glosses over the fact that there has been great dissension in the Church from the very beginning. We read of the first big row in the Church in the Acts of the Apostles, and I want to suggest that attention to the nature and terms of that disagreement can be very illuminating for us in our present discussions concerning human sexuality.

The disagreement concerned the extent to which the Hebrew Scriptures, what Christians refer to as the Old Testament, should be interpreted as they always had been. It centred on the demands of the law in the light of the Christ event and culminated with the 'liberal' Paul persuading the 'conservative' James at the Council of Jerusalem of AD 48–50 – about which we read in Acts 15 –

that Scripture should be reinterpreted. This first big dissension took place fewer than 30 years after the crucifixion and resurrection of Jesus when some of the original followers of Jesus were still alive.

We can learn much more about what was going on by paying close attention to Paul's Letter to the Galatians. A mere glance at the text makes it clear that there was a row going on. Paul is angry. He calls them 'you foolish Galatians' (Gal. 3.1) and utters threats against his unnamed conservative adversaries: 'let that one be accursed!' (Gal. 1.8). He goes so far as to say that he wishes those who were unsettling his readers would castrate themselves (Gal. 5.12).

Paul's adversaries argued that all converts, whether they were Jewish or Gentile, must accept and apply the Scriptures in the same way as they had always been because they contained authoritative rules for Christians and could not be modified or adjusted. The argument was in essence about what the Christian life should look like. That depends, as it does in today's argument over sexuality, on what you believe about God and what God requires of us as Christians.

If Paul's opponents had won the day, all male converts would have had to be circumcised and all Christians would have had to keep the law of Moses as set out in the Pentateuch, the first five books of the Bible. They would have been prohibited from eating food that was 'unclean', obliged to keep the sabbath and submit to many other strictures. In sum, Christianity would have remained a Jewish sect.

Paul is upset because his converts were doing just that: 'You are observing special days, and months, and seasons' (Gal. 4.10). It seems that they were happy to do so – otherwise Paul would not have had to write to them as he did and would not have been so angry with those who were encouraging them. Why did they succumb to these regulations? Probably because it made them feel safe: it made them feel that they had roots, with Abraham as their father and Sarah as their mother; it enabled them to think of themselves as privileged insiders, with genealogy and status.

'IN CHRIST'

It's easy for us to be puzzled by the readiness of the Galatians to submit to Paul's opponents but I suspect that if we had been among them we might well have been won over. Their argument might have appeared straightforward and persuasive, and Paul's rather arcane.

Paul's opponents could boast that they had Scripture on their side, that Scripture made it crystal clear what was necessary to belong to the people of God. God had said to Abraham: 'Any uncircumcised male who is not circumcised in the flesh of his foreskin shall be cut off from his people; he has broken my covenant' (Gen. 17.14).

Paul's opponents would have been able, further, to point out that Jesus had been circumcised (Luke 2.21), as had his followers. If they had kept the law, how could some of his followers not do so? Though St Matthew's Gospel would not have been available to St Paul, Jesus' words in it are hardly encouraging to Paul's case:

> Do not think that I have come to abolish the law or the prophets; I have come not to abolish but to fulfil. For truly I tell you, until heaven and earth pass away, not one letter, not one stroke of a letter, will pass from the law until all is accomplished. Therefore, whoever breaks one of the least of these commandments, and teaches others to do the same, will be called least in the kingdom of heaven. (Matt. 5.17–19)

If further argument were needed, Paul's opponents would probably have said that the church in Jerusalem should be the model for other churches. The 11 disciples had moved there after the resurrection and the leader of the church there was the Lord's brother James (as mentioned in Gal. 1.19, 2.9 and 12). They would all have been circumcised and observant Jews and the Church there seen as authoritative, the guardian of tradition.

Finally, although Galilee and Judea had large non-Jewish populations, there is little evidence that Jesus had much to do with them. In both the case of the Syrophoenician woman (Mark 7.24–30) and the centurion (Matt. 8.15–30) their non-Jewish status had been noted as exceptional and Jesus had not entered their houses. Jesus is recorded as saying: 'Go nowhere among the Gentiles' (Matt. 10.5).

The argument could well have run: 'If Jesus did not have dealings with Gentiles how can we go against him now? Surely Gentiles must become Jews to become part of the People of God. We have the Lord's practice as authority for this and nothing he said went against it.' This was the attitude of Peter as it is described in Acts 10 and 11. He and others came to regard associating with Gentiles and eating unclean food as a new freedom given by God revealed in the vision described in Acts 10.9–16.

We can easily underestimate the force of these arguments, which would have been very clear to Jewish people of the time. The Jews had fought and won a war in the second century BC, the Maccabean Revolt, in order to secure the right to keep the law in its entirety. It was a very live and toxic issue, as a glance at 1 Maccabees will make very clear.

Paul's opponents had a series of very convincing arguments. What were Paul's? The arguments were selective. He did not use Genesis 17.14, quoted above, which is so clear on the mandatory nature of circumcision; he uses Chapters 15—18 instead. Likewise, he does not quote Jesus.

Paul quotes Scripture frequently, maybe because that was what his opponents were doing and he therefore felt he needed to do the same, but his argument does not derive from or depend upon Scripture. He uses Scripture in the light of his faith, which depends upon something else. He elucidates his approach in 2 Corinthians: 'whenever Moses is read, a veil lies over their minds; but when one turns to the Lord, the veil is removed' (2 Cor. 3.15–16).

The crux of Paul's faith is that God has done, and is doing, a new thing in Jesus: in Jesus' birth and resurrection, but also thereafter in Paul's conversion from persecutor of the Church to apostle. Paul talks of his encounter with the leaders of the church in Jerusalem and what the Spirit did to the Galatians during his first visit (Gal. 3.4). Paul is demonstrating that God is now dealing with humanity differently.

'IN CHRIST'

By talking about all this Paul is asking his readers to reflect on the fact that they are in a new relationship with God through God's own initiative and action in Jesus (Gal. 4.9). The outcome of all this is that they, like all believers, have a new freedom that they had never known before. He therefore begs them not to return to where they were before they heard his preaching.

So, Paul is arguing not from Scripture, nor from tradition (represented here by the Jerusalem church) but, rather, he is making it clear that the Spirit is doing a new thing in Christ. The Letter to the Galatians is therefore of permanent value to the Church as a reminder of this and of the great freedom we have as Christians. The Church has gone on learning the profound implications since the time that Paul was writing to the Galatians and it is still doing so.

The new-found freedom we are called to enjoy in Christ has gradually been discovered and made manifest down the centuries. Paul spent his entire ministry fighting for the truth that in Christ there is no Jew nor Greek, aware though he might have been of the significance of the other assertions he made that in Christ there is no slave nor free, no male nor female. It took until the nineteenth century for the truth that in Christ there is no slave nor free to begin to be realized. Before that, Christians had quoted the Scriptures as an argument that supporting slavery was entirely proper and millions of people – Christian and non-Christians alike – suffered terribly as a result.

It's easy for us in retrospect to look back with amazement that Christians argued for the retention of slavery but it is a matter of historical record that Wilberforce and his colleagues had to fight tirelessly for its abolition against very strong resistance. So the truth that in Christ there is no slave nor free, of which Paul wrote to the Galatians, was not realized until some 1,800 years later.

The final truth of which Paul wrote in Galatians 3.28 – that in Christ there is no male nor female – only began to be tackled properly in the twentieth century. Universal suffrage was eventually won in the UK through Acts of Parliament in 1918 and 1928. Women were first ordained priests in the Church of

England in 1994 and bishops in 2015. It was a long and sometimes bitter battle.

Neither of these changes was achieved through the application of Scripture alone. They were achieved by the use of Scripture through the living tradition of the Church, bringing to bear reason and experience. Just as the New Testament takes slavery for granted, there are texts in Paul's writings that suggest that women should not be allowed to pray out loud in church, let alone be ordained – for example, Paul wrote about women not praying with their heads uncovered (1 Cor. 11.1–13) and not speaking in church (1 Cor. 4.34–35). It is well-nigh impossible to reconcile these passages with women taking an equal part in church worship, let alone be ordained. Taken at face value, these texts would mean all Christians who are female wearing head coverings in church or in prayer. The fact is that we all view the Scriptures through a particular lens. As Walter Brueggemann puts it:

> All interpretation filters the text through life experience of the interpreter. The latter is inescapable and cannot be avoided ... we read the text according to our vested interests. Sometimes we are aware of our vested interests, sometimes we are not. It is not difficult to see this process at work concerning gender issues in the Bible.[1]

This process enables some of us who would think of ourselves as 'Bible-believing Christians' to question what others would describe as 'the plain meaning of Scripture'. It is necessary to point to other texts and produce arguments to suggest that these should carry more weight. In fact, it is only when we look at these passages, together with what Paul says elsewhere about there being neither male nor female in Christ, that it becomes more difficult for Christians to use the texts to bolster patriarchy or even to subjugate women. As I have pointed out above, Paul used biblical texts selectively in his Letter to the Galatians.

Paul was not 'antinomian' – someone who is against any kind of law. He was selective, believing that the laws that separated

Jews from others were no longer to be observed. He wants his converts to experience the full freedom of the gospel: 'you were called to freedom, brothers and sisters' (Gal. 5.13), and to use their freedom in the service of others: 'do not use your freedom as an opportunity for self-indulgence, but through love become slaves to one another' (Gal. 5.13). He believed that 'the whole law is summed up in a single commandment, "You shall love your neighbour as yourself"' (Gal. 5.14, quoting Lev. 19.18).

In the twenty-first century we are coming to grips with another implication of the fact that in Christ there is no male nor female: that faithful monogamous same-sex relationships should be celebrated and supported, not prohibited. In so doing, we are discovering another freedom that has been denied for centuries but which, if we are to take the message of Paul to the Galatians seriously, must be given. God continues to do a new thing in Christ through the power of the Holy Spirit.

This process involves the application of the Scriptures through the living tradition of the Church, bringing to bear reason and experience. The latter is crucial here as we now know that, whether it is through nature or nurture, attraction to those of their own sex is not something that people choose. As a result, it can no longer be claimed that it is 'not natural'. It is.

The fact is that Christian teaching on marriage has varied greatly over the centuries, as Diarmaid MacCulloch makes clear in his magisterial *Lower than the Angels: A History of Sex and Christianity*. He summarizes:

> Many errors of understanding sex and Christianity have centred round complexities in the nature of marriage, not least the frequent assertions that there is something called 'traditional marriage' that needs defending against all competitors. This 'traditional marriage' tends to be the sort of companionate and carefully limited nuclear family that suits many people at the present day but has very little precedent in the history of the Church.[2]

Church history shows us a gradual realization of the radical freedom that Paul preached as we seek to apply the message of the New Testament, interpreted through the living tradition of the Church in the light of modern science to make a reality the proclamation of Paul to the Galatians that in Christ there is no Jew nor Greek, no slave nor free, no male nor female.

It is of course true to say that, elsewhere, Paul has nothing good to say about same-sex relations:

> It must be admitted that wherever instances of same-sex sexual activity are found in the Bible they are unequivocally condemned but what I believe the Bible condemns is something that every gay person in the Church today would also condemn – abusive, oppressive, exploitative relationships. The Bible never explains why same-sex sexual activity is condemned: it may well be the exploitative nature of the activity described. Leviticus 18 is a case in point and 1 Corinthians 6.9 is another. Both texts are difficult to translate with any certainty but one clue of how to do so may be the other vices on Paul's list. They are all examples of abusive, domineering, self-seeking, exploitative and even criminal behaviour, which are rightly condemned. Paul clearly has Leviticus in mind. (An open letter from Bishop John – Diocese of Worcester)[3]

As much as certain commentators would like to claim otherwise, it is far from clear that the so-called 'clobber texts' refer to consensual homosexual activity. There is, further, no good case to argue that the Scriptures in their entirety condemn or even consider consensual homosexual activity, any more than they give us a clear steer on many modern questions – like contraception and AI.

In any case, a narrow literalist biblical theology tends to put all the emphasis upon sexual acts whereas Christians, of all people, ought to recognize that relationships between people are more than that. The Common Worship Marriage Service begins with a sentence from 1 John: 'Those who live in love live in God and God lives in them.' That is as true of gay people in faithful monogamous relationships as it is straight people. Let us demonstrate that to them.

In sum, God has revealed Godself in Jesus and continues, in the power of the Holy Spirit, to do a new thing in exactly the manner that Paul pointed out to the Galatians. The Galatians, to his disappointment and frustration, were sorely tempted to continue to be imprisoned in their former straightjackets. Now is the time for us to enable gay people to celebrate their God-given identity as a gift to the Church, and not a problem for it. We should be encouraging them to enter into monogamous faithful relationships in exactly the manner in which we do straight people, and cease denying them their full humanity since in Christ there is no longer Jew nor Greek, no longer slave nor free, no longer male nor female, since all are one in Christ.

Notes

1 See https://www.outreach.faith/2022/09/walter-brueggemann-how-to-read-the-bible-on-homosexuality/ (accessed 07.03.25).

2 Diarmaid MacCulloch, 2018, *Lower than the Angels: A History of Sex and Christianity*, London: Penguin, p. 491.

3 See https://www.worcester.org.uk (accessed 07.03.25).

PART 3

Creation

5

Kingdom-shaped Love

OLIVIA GRAHAM

Introduction

The last half century has seen an extraordinary and rapid change in attitudes towards sexual matters and norms. Within the Church of England, some previously held negative attitudes (for example, towards illegitimacy, remarriage after divorce, contraception) have been widely discarded, while questions about gender and same-sex relationships are more prominent now than at any time in the Church's history.

Questions around love and sex have pushed many in our churches into anxiety, fear and rage – either because of the fear of discarding the traditional teaching of the Church on these matters and losing our anchorage, or because of a searing sense of injustice and cruelty caused by a second-class status being ascribed to sexual minorities.

The Church of England is no stranger to the task of holding together very disparate views. We were formed in the crucible of fierce disagreement about the nature of the Eucharist in times of reformation and churn in Christendom. We represent a marriage between Protestants and Catholics, in which rumbling discontent has often been a feature, and open warfare erupts from time to time.

So the time is ripe for us to look again at what we, as a Church, teach about love, sex and marriage. There are many published articulations of traditional teaching. Here we move towards articulating a new approach that takes account of Scripture, the tradition of the faith, and our developing and deepening understanding of the wonder and complexity of Creation, including humankind.

In the New Testament, Jesus condemned hypocrisy and greed, but was silent on homosexuality, and notably forgiving on sexual sin. After Jesus, Christian opinions, neuroses and obsessions around questions of sex, marriage and gender were formed among a rather small number of male theologians, and then hardened into 'doctrine' (the definition of which remains in dispute). Many variables were at play during this process, including male perspectives on women, and the tendency of some believers to treat metaphor as fact.

Creation

Let's start at the very beginning. In the beginning, Scripture tells us, was chaos and darkness. And the power of Creation, the breath (*ruach*) of God hovering over the waters, poised (Gen. 1.1–2). In the beginning also was the Word. The Word was with the Creator from the beginning (John 1), and presided with the Creator over the separation of the darkness from the light; the sky from the earth; the land from the sea. The Word was with the Creator when the earth began to produce the vast diversity and variety of plant and animal life, woven together in a complex adaptive system made up of interconnected ecosystems, with all life depending on the Creator and the Word for its origin, and dependence on each other part of it for its growth, flourishing and continuation.

And then the Creator and the Word brought humans of both genders into existence, made in God's image, breathed with life. God saw everything that God had made, and it was very good. This is the story of Creation we have received through our Scriptures. Not a literal account of physical and chemical processes, but a theological narrative that explains not the how, but the why. And it tells us a great deal about the nature and meaning of things.

Creation is vast and beautiful and complex. Relationship is built into it: what affects one part of it affects other parts. Dependencies are everywhere. The ability to grow and reproduce is built into it through sexual or asexual activity. Throughout the animal and plant kingdoms there are norms, and there are variations, and there is adaptation according to environment and circumstance.

The book of Genesis tells us that God created male and female, and that sexual activity between them was the norm, leading to the creation of a family unit and the gift of children. Throughout human history, this has been marked by ceremonies – betrothal, marriage, covenanting. Throughout human history it has been viewed in different ways, but generally with the female as an inferior, without much agency, whose sexuality must be controlled in order that ownership of property, land, inheritance and family lines are kept intact.

The Bible gives us examples of six different ways in which sexual bonding has been normalized, in addition to the nuclear family found in Genesis 2.24 – polygamy, concubinage, Levirate marriage, forced marriage to one's rapist, intercourse with the wife's female slave(s), ownership (and rape) of female prisoners of war. God does not appear to condemn any of these forms of marriage or family structures. 'Biblical marriage' is therefore a somewhat tricky concept. But we do have, in the Genesis narrative, a man and a woman, who join together and found a race.

Throughout history, too, there have been variations on sexual norms. Most people are wired for heterosexual relationships leading to procreation, and this is the norm reflected in the Genesis narrative. But a small percentage of the human population has always experienced life differently, with a number of variants: same-sex attraction, attraction to both sexes, no sexual attraction. In addition, some people are born with indeterminate sexual characteristics, and the allocation of gender has been difficult. The term 'eunuch' in the Bible describes this condition, as well as being applied to those who have been castrated and those who abstain from marrying (voluntary celibates), as Jesus explained in Matthew 19.12. From this we may deduce that Jesus would have considered himself a eunuch. The treatment and place of eunuchs in the societies of the Old Testament in relation to the law of Moses was not a matter for uniform agreement. The Old Testament has at least two very different perspectives on how eunuchs should be treated. In Isaiah 56.4 they are given an honoured place in God's house, while in Deuteronomy 23.1 they are excluded from the assembly, along with those born outside of marriage; and in Leviticus 21.20 they are lumped together with those who have any kind of disability, and are forbidden from approaching the altar in case they profane the sanctuary. So we can say that God made them, male and female. But apparently it wasn't quite so simple.

Naturally occurring variation is not restricted to human beings. It is also found in the animal kingdom, and same-sex sexual activity has been observed in over 1,500 species, including mammals, birds, reptiles and insects. In many species, this behaviour strengthens social bonds and facilitates group cohesion and conflict resolution.[1]

When Christians say that God created the world and all that is in it, we do not mean that God waved a magic wand and it appeared. We generally mean that God is somehow the Origin of a fantastically complex process of evolution and adaptation, which has enabled the rich diversity of life on this planet to exist. And it is all good. The biblical account emphasizes that we are all created in the image of God (Imago Dei). This foundational belief is written into international human rights law, which is based on our Western Judeo-Christian heritage, underscoring the inherent dignity, worth and equal value of every person. This includes the recognition of every variant in sexual make-up and orientation, in the same way that it treats other characteristics – race, (dis)ability, neurodiversity and so forth.

Inclusion

Jesus considered inclusion to be a good of the highest order – in fact, his top trump. He knew that his outrageous inclusion would foment disunity ('I come to bring not peace but a sword',

Matt. 10.34f.). Yet he ate and drank with 'sinners' and those who were ritually unclean (Luke 7.34); he violated the Law, healing on the Sabbath (Mark 3.1–6); he healed and exorcised all who came to him because that was core to who he was; he chose the marginalized over the respectable and law-abiding, and he never administered a test of orthodoxy or purity. He chose a tax-collector and a Zealot to be among his very closest friends. And in all this, the medium was the message: he showed us by the way he was, as well as what he taught, the very nature of God, the One in whose image we are made.

It was not that Jesus considered that 'anything goes'. Among the many behaviours he condemned were hypocrisy (Matt. 23), greed (Luke 12.15), and judgmental attitudes (Matt. 7.1–5). He preached a gospel of grace, compassion, and the overriding primacy of Love as the identity of God and the power of God. This understanding of God is read back into our appreciation of the whole arc of Scripture with its gradual, incremental understanding of Love as the power behind the creation of all that is, and its recurrent themes of justice, compassion and grace.

God's gift of diversity

We can't purge the world of its beautiful, breathtaking and crazy variety. And why would we want to? It is God's gift to us. And nor should we try to force people against their nature into narrow templates of behaviour that countermand Jesus' own joyful embrace of human variety. Human sexuality is not a choice between right and wrong. It is our embodied experience of the way we are – each of us 'fearfully and wonderfully made' as the Psalmist reminds us, each of us made in the image of God.

The parable of the wheat and the tares (Matt. 13.24–30) is a beautiful, nature-based account of who we are; and it tells us that we are not the ones to judge. Nature produces all kinds of growth in great variety, in spite of our efforts to control it. The roots of the plants that are seeded by human hand, and those that spring up naturally, are intertwined. As we learn more and more about mycorrhizal networks and the connection and interdependence of different species in ecological zones, we realize that we understand less and less. Our task is not, by harsh judgements, to foreclose on God's grace and mercy, ripping through delicate complexities which we have only a partial understanding of. We can, in trust, leave it to God to sort out the detail when the final account comes in.

So drawing on our growing understanding of the God-given diversity found in the natural world, including our species, we turn to an expanded understanding of the nature of sexual love, sexual ethics and our treatment of marriage.

Created for relationship

We are beings who are created for relationship ('It is not good that the [human] should be alone', Gen. 2.18). Most of us are created to be attracted to the opposite sex. Some of us are created to be attracted to our own sex. A very few of us have been given the gift of celibacy. So we may ask why would a good and loving Creator make people who yearn for affection and intimacy, and then forbid them from finding it with those they are wired to be attracted to? If we say, in answer to this question, that a good and loving Creator would not lay such a cruel burden on God's beloved humans, then this brings us to a new place when we consider the 'goods' of relationships that are not heterosexual marriage, but that are nevertheless characterized by mutuality, respect and self-giving love – because it is in these things that we find reflections of Divine love, and anticipatory signs of the kingdom of God.

Human relationships are complex; fairy-tale marriages are generally only found in fairy tales. But we recognize good fruit when we see it, and in relationship terms we can tell a healthy, respectful and loving relationship from a controlling and abusive one. Jesus gave a clear steer on the importance of fidelity, chastity and lifelong commitment in his teaching about divorce (Matt. 19.3–9). These are the intentions we should be looking for in relationships that come to the Church for affirmation and blessing.

The development of teaching

We have changed our teaching on sexuality and associated ethical and relational issues many, many times over the years, as our developing understanding and our social context have worked in union with the way we read the biblical text. Here are some examples:

- *Should clergy be allowed to marry?* The Christian Churches have taken varying approaches to this question over the centuries, and it is again a hot topic in the Roman Catholic Church for the pragmatic reason that there is a serious shortage of young men willing to commit to celibacy on ordination.
- *Is it ever permissible for a Christian man to have more than one wife?* Not usually, no. But in 1855 Bishop John Colenso found that the missionaries under his care in South Africa were requiring polygamous men to cast off all but one of their wives before they could receive baptism (leaving the surplus wives and children with no household or means of support). Colenso found this requirement unwarranted by Scripture, opposed to the practice of the apostles, condemned by common reason, and altogether unjustifiable.[2] The debate over it raged in the Anglican Church for a century. The 1888 Lambeth Conference rejected the call for a pastoral accommodation; 100 years later, Resolution 26 recommended that polygamists could be baptized and confirmed so long as they did not enter new marriages.
- *What about contraception?* In 1920 the Lambeth Conference rejected the use of contraception, even within marriage. The 1930 Conference gave qualified support to it. Today it is accepted in most (but not all) Christian denominations.

- *And how about marriage to a deceased wife's sister?* It was once a strongly held view in the Church that maintaining the Victorian prohibition against this was absolutely necessary in order to protect the laws of marriage and chastity, and it was hotly debated throughout the nineteenth century. The 1907 Act that removed this prohibition also allowed for clergy to refuse, on grounds of conscience, to officiate at such a wedding as long as they nominated a substitute clergyman in the same diocese. Today we would be hard put to find anyone who still thought that such a marriage was incestuous, or find a clergyperson who refused to conduct such a wedding.

- *Is divorce ever allowed, even though Jesus specifically condemned it?* The Church of England adjusted its teaching on the permanence of marriage in 2002 by adding a footnote to Canon B30 to enable clergy to remarry divorced people, with a spouse still living, after proper enquiry. It also provided for clergy to decline to do this on grounds of conscience.

All of these have been live (and very hotly debated) issues for Christians.

Embodied

We are created with bodies, enfleshed, one unit – body, mind and spirit. The dualism of the Platonic philosophy (body = bad, to be subdued and disciplined; mind/spirit = higher and more noble, to be cultivated) is not borne out by what we understand from the Scriptures about God's purpose and design in our creation. Indeed, it could be argued that the Christian pilgrimage is one of integration, of becoming comfortable in one's skin, with who we are, warts and all, knowing that we are loved and redeemable.

In the Michael Harding Memorial Address 'The Body's Grace', Rowan Williams suggests that grace, for the Christian believer, is a transformation that depends in large part on knowing ourselves to be seen in a certain way: as significant, as wanted. He says:

The whole story of creation, incarnation and our incorporation into the fellowship of Christ's body tells us that God desires us, as if we were God, as if we were that unconditional response to God's giving that God's self makes in the life of the Trinity. We are created so that we may be caught up in this; so that we may grow into the wholehearted love of God by learning that God loves us as God loves God.[3]

He goes on:

When we bless sexual unions, we give them a life, a reality, not dependent on the contingent thoughts and feelings of the people involved, true; but we do this so that they may have a certain freedom to 'take time', to mature and become as profoundly nurturing as they can. If this blessing becomes a curse or an empty formality, it is both wicked and useless to hold up the sexuality of the canonically married heterosexual as absolute, exclusive and ideal.

Williams argues that to be formed in our humanity by the loving delight of another is an experience whose contours we can identify most clearly and hopefully if we have also learned, or are learning, about being the object of the causeless loving delight of God, being the object of God's love for God through incorporation into the community of God's Spirit and the taking-on of the identity of God's child.

He also suggests that in a Church that accepts the legitimacy of contraception, the absolute condemnation of same-sex relations of intimacy must rely either on an abstract fundamentalist deployment of a number of very ambiguous texts, or on a problematic and non-scriptural theory about natural complementarity, applied narrowly and crudely to physical differentiation without regard to psychological structures.

Human experience and desire

The relational nature of our Trinitarian God serves as a model for all human relationships, including sexual and married relationships. Marriage, for Christians, is not just a social contract, or a means of procreation, but a covenantal relationship that mirrors the love and faithfulness of God. God is love, and those who live in love live in God and God lives in them (1 John 4.16). It is characterized by self-giving love, faithfulness, stability and the intention of permanence. At its best it is a force for good, enriching society and strengthening community (preface to the Common Worship marriage service).

This is an important perspective. We are right to take marriage seriously. It is the way of life, for those called to intimate relationship, that best enables us to flourish as human beings, and which best supports the flourishing of society through the stability that it gives. And for this reason, with this understanding, we need to change our prohibition on marrying same-sex couples in church.

Of course, the gospel makes clear that marriage is a human social arrangement, designated for human flourishing. It is not our ultimate destination, which is union with God. There is a qualitative distance between human social arrangements and the kingdom of heaven. And when we make the transition into the life beyond this one, the bonds of marriage no longer apply.

Jurgen Moltmann picks up this theme in his discussion of Christian hope. He says that hope is not just about personal individual salvation – it is about the redemption and renewal of the entire creation. Seen through this lens, all of our relationships should be oriented towards the coming kingdom of God, and characterized by justice, peace and mutual flourishing. In this light, the Church should support and bless relationships that embody these values, regardless of whether or not they fit traditional patterns.

Conclusion

Can God be offended by homosexuality, when it is clearly a naturally occurring variant on our God-given nature? And can God be offended by his beloved humans who are attracted to their own sex, seeking love and intimacy? I think not.

Homosexuality manifested in stable, loving, permanent, faithful relationships is not what the Bible condemns in the oft-quoted 'clobber texts'. These speak of relationships that are potentially abusive, coercive, violent, unloving and disrespectful, and God is surely offended by them. These we must stand against and call out when we find them.

But let us affirm our sexuality as an integral part of our human identity, created by God, and understood within the context of God's overarching purposes for humanity, and as a means of experiencing and sharing God's grace. It is time to change the teaching of our Church on marriage.

Notes

1 See, for example, J. M. Gómez, A. Gónzalez-Megíasand and M. Verdú, 'The evolution of same-sex sexual behaviour in mammals', *Nature Communications*, 14.5719 (2023), at https://doi.org/10.1038/s41467-023-41290-x (accessed 07.03.25).

2 John William Colenso, 1855, *Remarks on the Proper Treatment of Cases of Polygamy as Found Already Existing in Converts from Heathenism*, Pietermaritzburg: May and Davis.

3 Rowan Williams, 1989, 'The Body's Grace' (Michael Harding Memorial Address), Nottingham: Lesbian and Gay Christian Movement.

6

You Made Me This Way Because You Wanted One Like Me: Reflections on Sexuality and Creation

SAMUEL WELLS

The intriguingly named Kinky Friedman, a Jewish singer/songwriter, ran as an Independent for Governor of Texas in 2006. He was asked about his views on same-sex marriage. He replied, 'I support gay marriage. I believe they have a right to be as miserable as the rest of us.' Before we speculate about what his wife thought of his remarks, it's worth knowing that Kinky has never, in fact, been married. Nonetheless, his comment highlights the anomaly at the heart of the same-sex marriage debate: surely it isn't in God's character to create one group of people such that they are central to God's purposes while another group of people are invalidated from fulfilling God's purposes? Isn't that the approach God moved away from in the embrace of the Gentiles narrated in the Acts of the Apostles? The Bible seems clear on the matter.

It seems we need to revisit what God's Creation was about in the first place.

Created for relationship

In John 17, Jesus describes how the persons of the Trinity glorified one another before the world existed. The Trinity dwelt in the wonder of essence before there ever was existence. So why did existence come about? It came about so the Trinity could share beyond itself the glory of coexistence – the mutuality and reciprocity of being with one another that is the purpose and fulfilment of all things. But here's the subtle point: the reason for existence – the cause of Creation – was that God might be with us in Christ: that Christ might share with humankind the 'being with' he shares with the Father and the Holy Spirit.

This means Christ didn't come to fix the results of the Fall – humankind's sin and death problem. Christ would have come regardless of the Fall, because Christ came not to rescue us but to fulfil the purpose of Creation – that God be with us. That purpose was utterly realized in Christ's Nativity – his helpless presence in our midst; and definitively embodied in his Crucifixion – the visible proof of God's desire to be with us come what may. The indestructibility of that purpose was made manifest in Christ's Resurrection, which showed that sin and death cannot ultimately separate us from God. Meanwhile, the Ascension shows that Christ being with us does not mean he does not remain part of the Trinity. Pentecost fulfils Christ's promise to be with us always, to the end of time, through the Holy Spirit. On the last day, all of Creation will, like Christ, revert from passing existence to eternal essence, and be with God forever. That is the ultimate purpose for which Creation was made. We exist to be with God, ourselves, one another, and the wider Creation now and for ever.

The significance of *being with* as a theological framework is that it constitutes a single continuous thread from Trinity through Creation, Incarnation, to Cross and Resurrection, and ultimately to heaven. Trinity is God being with God; Incarnation is God being with us; Creation is God creating a theatre for God to be with us; the Cross is God being with us whatever befalls; the Resurrection is the indestructibility of God being with us; and heaven is our being with God for ever. It is one seamless whole. Only in this context does the purpose of God creating the universe make sense. Thus Creation is not an event or a doctrine that has meaning or coherence outside its relationship to this sequence. Creation derives its significance from the way it embodies and facilitates the other parts of this story.

This version of Christianity is notable for the following reasons. It is a story about God that centres on Jesus rather than a story about us that centres on our guilt-and-mortality predicament. It is a story of abundance that foregrounds the flourishing of all, not a tale of scarcity that focuses on the rescue of some. It is a story that displays the wonder of God in Christ, rather than treating Jesus as an instrument commissioned to deliver human immortality. And, most importantly, it is a story in which God's means and God's ends are identical. Thus there can be no hint of 'We don't know why God requires us to keep this law but we do so anyway'; because everything God asks of us must be true to God's character.

If our hope is to be with God, one another and the wider Creation eternally, then our calling is to embody that hope in our contemporary relations. Thus does doctrine – in this case, eschatology, or God's future – translate into ethics – living God's future now. Our calling is not to try to imitate some 'original pattern' of how human life should be. This is for four reasons:

1 What matters is not where we're coming from but where we're going: Christian ethics is fundamentally eschatological, because it strives to embody today the way things will be for ever – not to repristinate an ideal of how things once were.
2 'The way things are' is revealed not in how they originally were, but in what we see in Jesus. Jesus is the definitive embodiment of God being with us and our being with God and with one another. Jesus precedes, transcends and is the raison d'être of creation.
3 Whether one thinks of the Fall as a historical event or as a way of talking about the flawed nature of existence, it's clear that no adherence to some kind of creation ordinance offers any guarantee of faithful discipleship and/or flourishing life. We have no access to some idealized creation era; but we do see Jesus, and we focus our energies on inhabiting the realm he embodies and inaugurates.
4 The doctrine and ethics of creation has still not fully found an angle of repose amid the turbulence of cosmological and evo-

lutionary science. Therefore, all the more reason to focus not so much on a posited original condition as on God's unfolding purpose.

Christian ethics is not about reverting to some preordained shape of life or conforming to the givens of existence; it is about aligning our lives with the character of God revealed in Christ and anticipating the relations with one another we will share in the wonder of eternal essence. In so doing we are aligning ourselves not with something extraneous but with our own flourishing, our truest self, who we really are, the indwelling Holy Spirit or Christ within.

Contracting and abiding

How exactly do we live God's future now? It's one thing to say *being with* is the seamless cord that runs through the Trinity, Incarnation, Creation, Cross, Resurrection and heaven. It's quite another thing to explore how *being with* is faithfully to be embodied in human relationships – intimate, familial, cordial, civil and across significant divides of distance, disadvantage or discord. For this treatment we may set aside most of these categories and focus on the first two; but before doing so we may pause and reflect on the theme that covers all of them: and that is covenant.

I suggest the different parties in the debate about same-sex marriage are working with different notions of what is meant by covenant. On the one hand, we have an account of covenant that sees it as more or less a contract: it sets out the rules by which humankind is to live, broadly outlined in the Ten Commandments and the Torah, modulated by the Sermon on the Mount, and the New Testament more generally. In return for the keeping of these strictures, God promises flourishing in this life and joy perpetual in the life to come. Given that adhering strictly to all these rules – particularly the Sermon on the Mount, with its injunctions not to say 'You fool!', or look with lust, or to assert one's view any more strongly than with the words 'Yes' and 'No'

– is beyond everyone, then forgiveness is available to the repentant sinner.

On the other hand, we have an account of covenant that is less specific about rules but more focused on relationship, in the spirit of the invitation 'Abide'. Here the words 'Abide with us', spoken by the two disciples to Jesus on the road to Emmaus story and transposed by the famous hymn into the first-person singular, become an invitation extended by the risen Jesus to all God's children: 'Abide with me.' The threat of eternal damnation no longer lurks as the consequence of transgression; the motivation for upholding the covenant is no longer to avoid hell or to reach heaven, but to enjoy relationship with God in Christ and the Holy Spirit. The question of the disciple is no longer 'What is my physical being shaped to do?' or 'What am I instructed to do?' but 'How can the way I relate to others inhabit the mutuality and reciprocity embodied in Jesus and anticipate the way we shall be with God, ourselves, one another and the renewed Creation for ever?' The whole equation of behaviour rewarded by blessing or punished by curse is taken out of the picture and replaced by genuine relationship of delight, partnership and enjoyment. The dynamic is less sticking (or returning) to the original plan and more discovering together what faithfulness means in new situations while facing new challenges. Covenant is founded not on fear but trust.

If we examine these two notions of covenant more closely, we can see how they represent rival understandings of what it means to be a faithful Christian – and thus why different sides of the sexuality debate can with integrity claim theirs is the righteous path. For the 'contract' group, God sets out the rules of the relationship; the Bible describes the way God establishes, renews and expands that contract, outlines the details of that contract, narrates the lengths to which God goes to restore that contract, and demonstrates the cost of our not keeping that contract. If one takes a particular strand of discourse about marriage through the Old and New Testaments, and reads the verses that seem to refer to same-sex intimacy as specific prohibitions, then this view of contract validates an assumption that rules out physical same-sex intimacy in any circumstances.

Those seeking to embrace a more generous understanding of same-sex relationships have tended to argue on three grounds.

1 *Inconsistency*: it is pointed out that strict scriptural prohibitions on such matters as usury, further marriage after divorce, female headship, killing, eating pork or shellfish, and personal wealth seem to be more easily set aside.
2 *Irrationality*: ethical prohibitions generally work on the principle that we should not harm one another and should seek only one another's flourishing; there are thus no grounds to uphold a ban on relationships that (simply by being same-sex) seem to cause no harm and often do untold good.
3 *Anachrony*: the first century understood the physical expression of same-sex eroticism only in oppressive terms and had no notion of mutual and respectful such relations; it also assumed child-rearing as a duty and ordered its life in households centred on patriarchy: whereas today the whole social configuration has changed, and conceiving and rearing children is a choice for some rather than a necessity for all. Thus to impose prohibitions based on first-century assumptions is absurdly anachronistic.

Compelling as these three arguments may be, what I want to point out is that they all accept the contract model – that faithfulness means adhering to the rules and being rewarded (or avoiding punishment) for having done so. Proponents of these arguments differ from traditionalists about which rules it makes sense to uphold. Such arguments will only ever be able to establish same-sex marriage as a legitimate exception; and never be able to articulate it as a positive blessing.

Let's now turn to the model I described above when citing the hymn 'Abide with me'. The abiding model is not fundamentally based around rule-keeping. This is not a deontological ethic that says actions are inherently right or wrong. Neither is it a divine command ethic that supposes it can precisely identify God's rules in every situation, and must advocate those rules regardless of whether they seem true to God's character or appropriate in a given context. Instead, it's a teleological approach: rather than looking back, to enquire, 'What do the instructions say?' it looks forward, to ask, 'What forms of life most aptly advance and anticipate the way we are with God, ourselves, one another and the wider Creation eternally?' Here the two questions that most matter are, 'What habits and practices will build up the Church most faithfully to reflect and enjoy the God-who-created-all-things-to-be-with-us?', and, 'How in the strength of those habits and practices will the Church most faithfully enjoy and share in the Holy Spirit's way of being with the world?' If these are the two key questions, then every single activity of Christians is ripe for scrutiny as to how well it fits such a teleological purpose; but what is immediately clear is that to suggest same-sex physical relationships can't possibly advance those two goals is absurd.

I have argued elsewhere that while the contract model portrays ethics as the performance of a script, this abiding model more nearly resembles a process of improvisation. It moves from the question 'What must this be in order to conform to God's original design?' to the question 'What could this be in God's forthcoming realm?' This is what I call living God's future now. It doesn't ignore, suppress or exclude gifts (such as LGBTQ+ identity) that don't seem to figure in the original design as the Church has largely interpreted it in Scripture and tradition so far; it enjoys discovering how such gifts enhance the story, and sees such improvisations as the decisive moments when the Church displays its faithfulness and reflects God's imagination.

I'm not denying that many people take for granted that the contract model is the only way to understand ethics. Instead, I'm suggesting that the abiding model more accurately reflects the character and purpose of God, more exhilaratingly portrays the nature of discipleship, and more helpfully outlines how the Church is to live when it faces contrasting convictions of what faithfulness entails.

Intimacy and nurture

We have seen that *being with* is the thread that runs through the character and purpose of God (doctrine). And we have seen that every time we form, establish, restore and deepen tender, understanding, gentle, humble relationship with one another, we imitate and anticipate the way God seeks to be with us, and glimpse the glory of eternity (ethics).

What, then, is marriage, except two people forming, establishing, restoring and deepening tender, understanding, gentle, humble relationship with one another? Here's the humiliation of marriage: however intense and powerful our feelings are, and our sense of self-importance is, we remain tiny, pointless, transient specks in the inconceivable enormity of space-time existence. But here's the wonder of marriage: God's life is shaped around being in relationship with such tiny specks as us; and marriage is potentially the single most enduring and absorbing icon of what tender, understanding, gentle, humble relationship can be. What two people can discover in the depth of their intimacy and the heart of their reconciliation, and the texture of their trust and the revelation of their fragility and the delight of their playfulness, and the guts of their endurance is the most important thing we can find in life: it's the most abiding form of *being with* we can experience.

Yet here, as often in debates around sexuality, we run into the problem that embracing same-sex relationships is not bolting on a disruptive and unhelpful additional dimension to the established and well-understood notion of marriage; for marriage is far from being a stable, simple or uncomplicated notion.

The New Testament presents two fundamental, but not identical, accounts of discipleship. One is individual: deny yourself, take up your cross, and follow me. The other is collective: you are the body of Christ. The fact that we seldom acknowledge in theory but face every day in practice is this: marriage doesn't fit comfortably into either model. It doesn't clearly resemble the individual model (singleness) or the collective model (the body of Christ, or the Church). The basic goods of marriage are care for the vulnerable and intimate companionship. Nurture of children and care for elders inhibit one's availability to be with Christ in individual, sacrificial itinerancy; meanwhile, the trust inherent in true intimacy and the depth required for genuine companionship are not things that can beneficially be shared liberally across a human community.

Thus it seems the creation character of marriage cuts across the gospel character of individual and collective discipleship. This is not a radical new challenge of the modern world: it has always been so. Same-sex marriage doesn't disrupt a settled and established pattern of how Christians faithfully honour personal vocation and ecclesial commitment; instead, it adds a new texture to an already complex picture.

Moreover, Jesus gives an unequivocal response to the Sadducees: 'in the resurrection they neither marry nor are given in marriage' (Matt. 22.30). So while in heaven there is being with God, on an individual level, and being with God and one another, in a corporate sense, it seems there is no separate, intimate, discrete, secluded relationship behind closed doors. Which suggests such relationships should not have today the exalted status they tend to be given by both sides in the same-sex marriage debate. Marriage sits easily within neither a temporal notion of discipleship nor an eternal picture of *being with*. Surely this must lower the stakes on all sides. Same-sex marriage is not confusing or discrediting the highly exalted status of marriage; it's catalysing a closer examination of whether marriage should ever have had such a highly exalted status.

Once we have reasserted that our principal calling is to be with God and one another, and that our primary ways of being with one another are as church together with God, and as church collectively with the world, we have put marriage in its place: not as an end in itself, not as a litmus test of conformity or faithfulness, but as one form of life (among many) that may or may not advance these prior forms of *being with* – but not the only or essential way. So we cannot configure the conversation as those who have attained the lofty heights of traditional marriage looking down to permit or prohibit other forms of coupling; still less as those who have apparently conformed to conventional models dictating God's will to those they judge not to be so conformed. Instead, we need to reckon with two forms of *being with* that marriage seems uniquely to embody, each of which seem to inhibit New Testament notions of individual or collective discipleship.

Those forms are erotic intimacy and care for the vulnerable.

Erotic intimacy is often dynamic yet potentially destructive. It yields untold joy but endless self-deception. To release its wonder, contain its power, and channel its fruits, world and church have long practised committed, lifelong, cherishing, companionable, exclusive relationships – invariably known as marriages.

Meanwhile, the raising of infants, and the care of the infirm and elderly, are too important to be outsourced entirely to third parties: while they inhibit freedom elsewhere, they constitute unique aspects of *being with*.

Perceived in these practical terms, it's hard to perceive any reason why marriages that advance these goals must be restricted to opposite-sex couples. These goals are so vital to human flourishing that a broader understanding of what marriage can mean, in the service of advancing these goals, is – on the contrary – very welcome indeed. Just as the Church has come to appreciate that in some cases a marriage is so damaging to these goals it is hardly a marriage at all, and would best be dissolved; and likewise, that parties to that marriage may advance those goals by finding another partner with whom to do so. So now, at long last, the Church may realize that these goals may be advanced at least as well by same-sex couples as by opposite-sex ones.

To amend Kinky Freeman, it is not that gay people have a right to be 'as miserable as the rest of us'. It's that the Church has a notion of marriage that has always sat uncomfortably with its two foundational accounts of discipleship; a sense of its calling that goes far beyond the particularities of domestic partnerships; and an ethic more exhilarating than a contractual adherence to specific rules. Given these three contexts, it has everything to gain from welcoming and celebrating the marriages of same-sex couples, and nothing to lose.

It's long past time that the Church ceased to regard the presence of LGBTQ+ persons as a troublesome deficit and celebrated it as an untold and unrecognized gift. And one of the many blessings arising from doing so might be a more honest, more integrated and more faithful understanding of marriage.

PART 4

Culture

7

Living in Love and Faith: The Failure of History

MARK CHAPMAN

One of the most interesting things about the 480 pages of *Living in Love and Faith* is just how little history it contains.[1] There is a lot about biblical interpretation – which proved highly contested and highly charged throughout the project – and a fair amount on scientific ways of understanding human beings and their complex sexual identity, but there is remarkably little on how institutions like marriage and understandings of human relationships and sexuality have developed through time. It should not have been like that: a whole study group was devoted to the examination of history. What gradually mutated into the Living in Love and Faith project[2] from the Bishops' Teaching Document began following the failure to 'take note' by the House of Clergy in General Synod of a somewhat ill-thought-out report on marriage in 2017: *Marriage and Same Sex Relationships after the Shared Conversations – A Report from the House of Bishops*.[3] This appeared to have been hastily drawn up and proposed no changes at all to the teaching on marriage, despite the lengthy period of so-called 'shared conversations' following the *Report of the House of Bishops' Working Group on Human Sexuality* produced by a group chaired by Sir Joseph Pilling, which had been set up in response to the legislation on same-sex marriage in England and Wales in 2013.[4]

One could be forgiven for thinking that the Church of England has spoken of little else other than sex through the 11 years of

Justin Welby's archiepiscopate. The response to the defeat of the 'take note debate' on the report in 2017 was to set up a large and well-funded study group to produce a new teaching document that surveyed scholarship and theology and pastoral practice in relation to sexual relationships. There were to be four working groups, one on the Bible, one on science, one on history, and one on pastoral practice alongside a co-ordinating group. None of these groups was easy to assemble. With the decimation of university theology over the past 50 years and the failure of the Church to invest in scholarship over many years, there simply was no pool of suitably qualified people who might have had the time to invest in the project. Furthermore, the different groups were chosen not simply for their academic credentials. They also represented something of the different views on the legitimacy or otherwise of same-sex relations across the Church of England. There was, as so often in the study of Church history, a conflict between scholarship and partisanship. To add to the complexity, it soon proved the case that the objectives were far from clear.

As a member of General Synod at the time, as well as having written on sexuality and the Anglican Communion, I received an invitation to become a member of the history group. The others were specialists in different periods of Church history: we had a classicist who was an expert in the history of gender and medicine in the ancient world, a Reformation scholar, a couple of modern historians, including me, and a historian of law. As well as a chair, there was also a staff member who acted as repetiteur. There were efforts to bring in a medievalist, although that never really materialized. In terms of doctrinal leanings within the Church there were a couple of evangelicals, one lay and one ordained, and three more or less liberal-minded, broadly catholic types (including me), two of whom were ordained. As far as I am aware, at least in the history group, we were never asked about our sexuality. During the course of the proceedings – which lasted a couple of years and which, when the project manager, the four groups and the steering group are added together, must have cost many hundreds of thousands of pounds in expenses and salary alone[5] – there were many short papers produced as well as detailed bibliographical resources which found their way on to a website, the 'LLF Learning Hub'.[6]

At the outset of the process there was no clear mandate about what was expected from the various groups. The only steer was that there was to be a new *Bishops' Teaching Document* on sexuality, marriage and relationships, although at first it was not evident whether this was meant as something proposing legislative changes in the light of new knowledge and research, or whether it was simply to be a lengthy discussion document to provide the academic background for possible future proposals that would be introduced by the bishops to General Synod in due time. However, because there were so many vociferous groupings in the Church for whom any change to the doctrine of marriage and sex was absolutely unthinkable, it soon became obvious that it could only ever be the latter. *Living in Love and Faith* was consequently to be a report on the current state of scholarship and pastoral practice.

The four groups were each convened by a bishop. It is not clear precisely what criteria had been used for the selection of the bishop convenors, especially as there were very few bishops who had expertise in any of the areas under discussion. In the history group, ours was the former Bishop of Winchester, Tim Dakin, whom I had known for many years, since we were both doing our doctorates in Oxford at the same time. He had been working on Karl Barth but left Oxford before he completed this to work in the Church Army College in Nairobi. This had been followed by a period as head of the Church Mission Society. At one of our early sessions at Church House Westminster, he introduced the meeting by asking whether the members of the history group might like to say what we thought about the question of same-sex relationships. We each looked at one another and realized that the answer was a polite but firm 'no'. We all felt that what any of us might think about the presenting issue was of little relevance to our work as historians. Most historians, perhaps rather naively, still like to believe in something like objective truth. We all got on very well and left others to have their fights. That said, despite the fact that our small group of historians worked hard during the long-drawn-out process to produce some solid resources, these were scarcely used in the final book. Fortunately, we now have Diarmaid MacCulloch's *Lower than the Angels*[7] which provides an admirable overview of some of the ways in which thinkers and churches have addressed human intimacy and the role of sex and sexuality through the whole course of Christian history.

From my experience of the wider discussions there were two areas that seemed to be particularly fraught. The first was the question of gender identity, and whose voices were to be included in the discussions. It became clear in the larger meetings where the groups met together that the goals of academic neutrality once again clashed with inclusion of advocates, which, of course, may well have been important but it is nevertheless a little different from the stated intention of a 'state of research' document. Second, of the four groups, it was the biblical group that seemed to have been most inclined towards a degree of internal hostility. Of course, good Anglicans will always want to see the Bible as containing all things necessary to salvation through faith in Jesus Christ, but that claim says nothing about how the Bible is to be used in ethical debate. It has been very clear that there was very little consensus about biblical authority among many of the contributors to the debate on same-sex relations.

The failure to embrace the work of the history group has meant that some of the historical assumptions that were made by the theologians and biblical scholars have been left almost unchallenged. Let me take just one example that comes from my own work on the contributions by the Church of England to the sexuality debate in the twentieth century. Once I had begun reading widely on the history of the Church of England and sexuality it quickly became clear to me that up until the 1970s, aside from a few general principles about love, there was remarkably little use of the Bible in discussions about sexual relations. Instead, as so often in the history of the Church of England, it was natural law that provided the substance for ethical debate. In general, the arguments that were used to defend the so-called traditional view of sexual relations between man and woman in marriage were very simple: the natural order of the universe was for there to be men and women. It was so ordered that their respective sexual organs fitted together and consequently every other form of sexual activity was therefore disordered. Furthermore, the chief point of sex was to procreate (even if there might be pleasurable side-effects). In turn, this natural ordering of sexual relations led to the institution of marriage in order to provide the offspring of such a marriage with a degree of financial and social security. This meant that for most of history, marriage was principally a set of financial transactions between families rather than anything particularly Christian.

The great problem with natural law, however, is that it can change if the understanding of nature changes: natural law has a history. Developments in the natural and human sciences could easily challenge the immutability of a universal natural law that applied to all people at all times. As soon as there was a recognition that some people are naturally attracted to people of the same sex, which some of the early sexologists called 'inversion', then the whole natural law argument could quickly come tumbling down. At the very least, empirical research required there to be a degree of nuancing in natural law arguments. If the natural condition of some was to be attracted to members of the same sex then surely this required a revision of the teaching on marriage and sexual relationships. And by the 1950s a substantial number of people accepted this – and even some in the Church began to call for legislative changes.

The Church of England's contribution began in earnest in 1952 when Graham Dowell, an ordinand at Ely Theological College who went on to become Vicar of Hampstead, wrote a letter to the influential journal *Theology*:

> Is homosexual concubinage to be treated purely and simply as an unio illicita like fornication and those who practise it to be judged as 'living in sin' and to be deprived of the sacraments of the Church? If so, what are we to say to those who profess to be congenitally homosexual?[8]

Dowell went on to ask for a Christian discussion of the penal code and that

> the Christian conscience should distinguish between promiscuity and fidelity, between the balanced union and the vicious perversion – between, in fact, the invert and the pervert: it should then examine both the justice and the expediency of a penal code which, far from curing or deterring the homosexual, has so often led to crime (particularly in the form of blackmail), to bravado, or to the tragedy of wrecked lives.[9]

At the request of Alec Vidler, the editor of *Theology*, Derek Sherwin Bailey of the Church of England's Moral Welfare Council responded to Dowell's challenge in an article in *Theology* published later in the year, where he argued for a calm approach to understanding the phenomenon of homosexuality of which 'sexual inversion' was not the only form.[10] Crucially, Bailey distinguished between what he called 'natural' inverts and 'those who have acquired a homosexual character or who have become addicted to homosexual practices'.[11] This debate in the pages of *Theology* led directly to the commissioning of a report from the Moral Welfare Council on *The Problem of Homosexuality*.[12] The responsibility of the Church was to understand homosexuality as thoroughly as possible: it could no longer be understood as something that could be cured like some sort of physical disease. The report, which was drafted by Bailey, and which was initially intended for private circulation but which was soon widely leaked, clearly identified homosexuality as a natural condition for a significant minority. This meant it was simply wrong to exercise legal punishment on people for doing what comes naturally.

Although a number of psychological explanations are proposed as to the causes of homosexuality, especially what it calls an 'unsatisfactory parental relationship',[13] the Report nevertheless suggests that 'inversion' is a condition that cannot be altered since there is no effective therapy. Principally for this reason, the report called for decriminalization. This was a somewhat momentous proposal. At the same time, it was also clear to Bailey that the Church should not adapt its teachings on sex as permissible only within marriage. He was unequivocal in continuing to regard homosexuality as a sin: 'Homosexual acts are sins against God, whether or not they are crimes against the State.'[14] Somewhat problematically, given that a natural law argument had been used to justify decriminalization, such sinfulness was also based on the natural-law argument that saw homosexuality as involving the 'unnatural use of non-complementary organs within a relationship which is not that of a man and woman'.[15] Christian inverts should consequently seek to 'accept their condition, and by seeking to sublimate their sexual lives in socially useful ways achieve personal fulfilment'.[16]

Perhaps rather naively, the Report suggested:

> In all cases of homosexuality the teacher should teach habits of self-control. He will stress the unnaturalness of homosexual physical intercourse and, more important still, help them to face their condition and sublimate or transmute their homosexual drives through prayer and imagination into creative and socially acceptable service such as youth leadership etc.[17]

This understanding of homosexuality as a sin meant that *The Problem of Homosexuality* – which resembles almost all subsequent Church of England teaching on homosexuality, including *Issues in Human Sexuality*, and even in the discussions around Prayers in Love and Faith – had a somewhat double-edged conclusion. The questions that Dowell had asked in his original letter as to whether 'homosexual concubinage' was to be regarded as 'living in sin' had been answered: the invert is exempt from being judged 'for his homosexual condition' which is morally neutral because it is natural,[18] but at the same time he cannot be absolved 'from responsibility for immoral homosexual practices' since it is also natural for genitals to be used in only one way.[19] Moreover, for Bailey, even if homosexuality were to be decriminalized it would still present a social problem and would be a sign of the breakdown of marriage and family life which were required to sustain human relations. The main task for Christians was consequently to improve family life so that 'inversion' does not happen in the first place – and here Bailey continued to suggest that homosexuality resulted primarily from problematic family relationships.

Bailey's overall conclusion was simple: what people did in private, provided it did not involve children or young adults, should not be a criminal offence, even though it remained a sin in the eyes of the Church. *The Problem of Homosexuality* consequently proposed decriminalization as a means that would help homosexuals find more equal relationships instead of having illicit liaisons, which it was thought might well involve children and adolescents. While this might not be wholly positive, it nevertheless meant that the Church of England was siding with reform of the criminal law.

Indeed, the Church of England was to become the principal contributor to the momentum that led to the Wolfenden Report. It was the Church that ensured that homosexuality and not just prostitution was discussed in the report. And it was the guarded support of the Church that allowed for the subsequent decriminalization of homosexual acts between men over 21 in private under the Labour government in 1967. This was undoubtedly a huge surprise to many. Writing in 1970, one commentator observed:

> there is the remarkable and usually unnoticed role of the Church of England as an active agent of change. In the last fifteen years or so its publications on such issues as homosexuality, abortion and illegitimacy have been well informed and judicious, essential reading for students and politicians alike; and they have all served to turn the moral flank of the opponents of change. Indeed, there would be truth – especially political truth – in the claim that the established Church is the putative father of 'the permissive society'.[20]

Similarly, Peter Wildeblood, the *Daily Mail* journalist jailed for 18 months in 1954 in a celebrated trial with Michael Pitt-Rivers and Edward Montagu (Lord Montagu of Beaulieu) for committing acts of indecency, could write in his memoirs:

> I had always thought of the Church as the last stronghold of prejudice and had never found an occasion for praising it for its courage in controversial matters; yet here, from Church House, came an attack on the law which was as broad-minded, clear-headed and brilliantly argued as one could wish. It was all the more surprising because the English laws against homosexuality were religious in origin and widely held to represent the views of the Church.[21]

That said, in the 1950s the Church expressed no desire to adapt its own teachings despite its recognition of the 'naturalness' of homosexuality and its support of decriminalization. Christian 'inverts' should consequently seek to 'accept their condition' and to sublimate it with celibacy and socially useful activity. Of course, all this is no surprise for the early 1950s, but celibacy and sublimation now seem both ludicrous and potentially dangerous for those who are not called to such states. And this may well be why from the 1970s, partly under the influence of American evangelicalism, many Christians started replacing what was increasingly understood as a discredited natural law theory with the even flimsier method of resorting to proof-texting scriptural passages ripped out of context.[22] It is clear that the Church was in many ways ahead of much of the wider society in the 1950s: decriminalization certainly did not have the support of other conservative institutions, including the Conservative Party. But it then stalled and forgot what Kenneth Ingram, one of its more forward-thinking authors, wrote in 1940 in a book published at the very beginning of World War Two and which was rapidly suppressed by William Temple. His words even seem remarkably biblical, and at the same time remind his readers that not all marriages meet the ideal:

> the love-motive is the only legitimate basis on which a positive sexual morality is likely to be built. Wherever there is

love, wherever the desire is genuinely mutual, there can be no immorality in sex ... Love is the test of sexual morality. Sex divorced from love, whether it occurs in a union which is officially designated as lawful marriage or not, belongs to an altogether lower level.[23]

The failed opportunity to learn from the past in *Living in Love and Faith* reveals that without a resort to the study of history the Church of England is perhaps destined to say the same thing over and over again while failing to note that few are any longer bothering to listen.

Notes

1 *Living in Love and Faith: Christian Teaching and Learning about Identity, Sexuality, Relationships and Marriage*, 2020, London: Church House Publishing.

2 See the website at https://www.churchofengland.org/resources/living-love-and-faith (accessed 07.03.25).

3 General Synod Document 2055. This remains online at http://www.tgdr.co.uk/documents/229P-GS2055.pdf (accessed 07.03.25).

4 *Report of the House of Bishops Working Group on Human Sexuality*, 2013, London: Church House Publishing.

5 No figures appear to have been published.

6 The 'LLF Learning Hub' at https://www.churchofengland.org/resources/living-love-and-faith/living-love-and-faith-learning-hub (accessed 07.03.25).

7 Diarmaid MacCulloch, 2024, *Lower than the Angels: A History of Sex and Christianity*, London: Penguin.

8 Graham Dowell, 'The Church and homosexuals', *Theology*, 55 (1952), 28–9, p. 28.

9 Graham Dowell, 1980, 'The Church and homosexuals', in Peter Coleman, *Christian Attitudes to Homosexuality*, London: SPCK, pp. 29, 162–3.

10 Derek Sherwin Bailey, 'The problem of sexual inversion', *Theology* 55.380 (1952), pp. 47–52.

11 Bailey, 'The problem of sexual inversion', p. 48.

12 Church of England Moral Welfare Council, 1954, *The Problem of Homosexuality: An Interim Report*, Oxford: Church Information Board.

13 Church of England, *The Problem*, pp. 10–12. This explanation was not uncommon at the time. The influential Michael Schofield (writing under the pseudonym Gordon Westwood), 1952, *Society and the Homosexual*, London: Victor Gollancz, had made similar claims.

14 Church of England, *The Problem*, p. 15.

15 Church of England, *The Problem*, p. 16. Interestingly, the report also condemns substitutes for coitus among married partners, p. 14.

16 Church of England, *The Problem*, p. 14.

17 Church of England, *The Problem*, p. 14.

18 Church of England, *The Problem*, p. 7.

19 Church of England, *The Problem*, p. 14.

20 O. R. McGregor, 'Equality, sexual values and permissive legislation: the English experience', *Journal of Social Policy*, 1 (1972), pp. 44–59, 56.

21 Peter Wildeblood, 1957, *Against the Law*, Harmondsworth: Penguin, p. 65. See also McGregor, 'Equality, sexual values', p. 56.

22 See, for example, Michael Green, David Holloway and David Watson, 1980, *The Church and Homosexuality: A Positive Answer to Current Questions*, London: Hodder and Stoughton.

23 Kenneth Ingram, 1940, *Sex-Morality Tomorrow*, London: Allen and Unwin, p. 168. On this, see Mark D. Chapman, 'Enjoying what comes naturally: the Church of England and sexuality in the 1930s', *Studies in Church History*, 60 (2024), pp. 453–76, 468.

8

Dare We Hold Together?

VIVIAN FAULL

I was ordained priest in the Church of God and the Church of England 30 years ago in 1994, one of the first generation of women to be priested. Of course, I knew from the start that parts of the Church of God could not – and would not – accept my priesthood, though I have always been received respectfully and often very warmly indeed in Roman Catholic and Orthodox churches. What has been much harder to live with is that there are those within the Church that ordained me who cannot accept my priesthood. For 20 years, as Dean first of Leicester Cathedral and then York Minster among many other duties, I made special liturgical arrangements for the ordinations of those who could not accept my own orders.

In 2018 I was consecrated Bishop of Bristol with oversight of its 200 parishes and communities, of which one large benefice and three smaller parishes are overseen spiritually by the Bishop of Oswestry. Several other parishes do not invite me to preach or teach (though I can invite myself, and try to do so tactfully and supportively). In May 2018 I committed myself to try to be bishop for everyone, and I have worked to maintain honest, strong and affectionate relationships with all those who identify as Anglicans, including those who do not support female bishops and, further, the vast majority of the 1 million people for whom I hold the cure of souls, who do not identify as Anglicans. This is a diocese in which anti-establishment and secular values are pervasive, and authority must be earned. I enjoy that task.

I have been supportive of the welcome of and full participation of lesbian and gay people in the Church of England for as long as I can remember, and throughout my time as a deaconess, priest and bishop. This became a matter of practical pastoral ministry as a university chaplain during the years when HIV emerged and the terror of that forged strong communities of sacrificial care for those infected, as scientists and physicians raced to discover and create treatments. I worked in cathedrals from 1990 and worked alongside – and cared for – staff and congregation members; I heard (as I had so often in Cambridge) searingly honest stories of discovery of sexual identity, of deep Christian vocation, and experiences of rejection by the Church.

When the Civil Partnership Act came into force in 2005, I was relieved that at last there was public recognition (and opportunity for celebration) of faithful, loving stable same-sex relationships but I was deeply concerned that some bishops regarded this meagre provision as a threat to heterosexual marriage and family life.

My own Christian journey included lengthy engagement with the variety of interpretations of biblical texts and debates with those who disagreed profoundly with my conclusions (and whose views I continue to respect). I was initially uncertain about the advisability of the Same Sex Marriage Act of 2013 and reviewed the changing history of English marriage law and custom. I knew, again from my experience of chaplaincy, that law and custom were continuing to change, not least for women and for those whose marriages had broken down. I was persuaded by my reading of the rightness of a further change to enable same-sex marriages to be recognized by the Church of England and I look forward with hope that the quadruple lock that currently bars us from celebrating same-sex marriages in the Church of England will become unclasped.[1]

But I remain bishop of a diocese where there are profound differences of opinion about the propriety of any same-sex sexual relationship and about any change to the Church's law on marriage. I have committed myself to being bishop for everyone.

How can I hold that tension?

DARE WE HOLD TOGETHER?

I have experienced how the Church seeks unity in diversity and disagreement. The diocese has one of the highest proportions of formal local ecumenical partnerships in the Church of England. The international commitment to church unity that gathered momentum in the early part of the twentieth century included among its leaders Oliver Tomkins, who became Assistant Secretary General of the World Council of Churches in formation in 1945. Oliver subsequently become Principal of Lincoln College and then Bishop of Bristol in 1959, remaining on the World Council of Churches central committee until his retirement in 1975. During his episcopate he oversaw the planting of churches into the rapidly expanding town of Swindon. Each church had an ecumenical foundation and governance.

I am in awe of Bishop Oliver's leadership (regarded by some as courageous and by others as foolhardy) and his determined inclusion of those with whom he differed theologically. He considered handing Bristol's cathedral, founded under Henry VIII in the former Augustinian monastic buildings, over to the Roman Catholic Diocese of Clifton which was then planning to build a cathedral to replace the inadequate proto-cathedral. The seat of the Anglican bishop would move to St Mary Redcliffe. However, the idea was gently rebuffed. Bishop Oliver was a courageous reformer, including in his championing the ordination of women. But he also reminds me that reform is complex and contested: he was surprisingly reluctant to support those striking for fair employment at the Bristol bus company, which operated a colour bar, and he never made his views clear on homosexuality. As I know well, there is only so much change that an organization can receive well, even at a time of hope for Church and nation. Bishop Oliver is buried in the cathedral garden, his grave marked with a simple headstone carved with his pastoral staff and the inscription 'May they all be one' (John 17.21).

So to return to the 30th anniversary of the ordination of women and to the use, during the decades of internal and ecumenical debate that preceded it, of that concept of receiving change well. Reception has become a useful concept in law and literature as ideas are transmitted and received (or not).

It has been picked up by theologians who noted that Creation receives its being from God; humanity receives God's revelation; Christ receives his mission from the Father; the Church receives its being from Christ – and all of this is brought about by an event of the Holy Spirit. In the earliest days of the Church, as we read in Acts, this reception was dynamic, reciprocal and uncertain, but that changed as the Church became institutionalized and hierarchical. Reception was identified by the way in which the decisions of the councils of the Church have over time (and sometimes a great deal of time) been absorbed – or not absorbed. Since the Reformation and renewal movements of the more recent Western Church, there have again been treasures shared from one tradition with another. The hymns of Charles Wesley, chants from Taizé and Iona, or the songs of Graham Kendrick and Matt Redman have transformed worship. The teaching of Pope Francis on the environment has influenced thinking across churches regardless of denominational boundaries.

And, since the nineteenth century, the changing self-understanding of women and the Church resulted in the formal doctrinal and legislative debates of the twentieth century in the Free Churches and, eventually, the Church of England. Increasingly, reception has come to be viewed relationally; not a political device for containing conflict but a quality, even a virtue, of being church. Reception is an aspect of being in communion, of partnership in the gospel which derives from being, as the Declaration of Assent puts it, 'part of the One, Holy, Catholic and Apostolic Church'. Part, not whole. And yet the Church of England claims its autonomy. In the words of the Declaration of Assent, the Church of England passes on what it has received, and proclaims those truths it has received afresh in each generation. Reception is a contextual and missiological concept.

Reception is relational. It depends on a recognition of our sisterhood and brotherhood in Christ, and on our recognition that we are baptized into one body, bound together on the Way (the fundamental concept of synodality), branches of the vine that is Christ.

The ordination of women to the priesthood became possible

politically only after the agreement in Synod and Parliament (indeed insisted on by some MPs) that there should be special arrangements, known as extended episcopal oversight, for those who, in conscience, could not accept the decision to ordain women. Some pushed further, for alternative episcopal oversight, perhaps in the form of an additional province alongside Canterbury and York; but after some years of argument (not least during the time of the Act of Synod) the Synod and Parliament agreed that this was unacceptable as a church within a Church. In 2014, in preparation for the first consecration of women as bishops, the House of Bishops set out Five Guiding Principles; these declare the full validity of women's ministry at all levels, and also declare that 'those who are unable to receive the ministry of women as bishops or priests have an assured place enabling them to flourish within the church'.

The problem is that, however determined and generous the relationships of mutuality, the assured place and sacramental provision of the Five Guiding Principles have solidified and ossified separation. Other than under the leadership of the most remarkable clergy and bishops, separate cultures have emerged, and bishops, particularly female bishops, find their ministries and identities undermined. To be a female priest or bishop in the Church of England is (for many) to internalize the sense that while our ministries continue to be restricted in law we are not yet regarded as fully human by the Church (as we are in much of the wider world, with great risk to our safety). And yet we continue to serve the Church of God in faith and hope and love.

In the Diocese of Bristol there are fences within the Church, and bridges from the Church linking us with other Christian communities. Our ecumenical relationships have become broader, to include, at least at the level of good relationships, community churches (many of which exist because of the inhospitable welcome to the Windrush arrivals, many of them Anglican). Relationships between church leaders are strong and supportive. But in my six years in the diocese the weight of governance structure required in local ecumenical partnerships has, with the time, cash and volunteer resources required, begun to overwhelm what had been lively diverse partnerships. Vision and energy have been lost, and two of the Swindon partnerships have agreed to end their formal ecumenical relationships while committing to continued friendships. The strong structures and heavy compliance obligations of Ecumenical Partnerships have tended not to lead to innovation but instead to stagnation, to death rather than life.

So to the current debate about the acknowledgement and welcome of same-sex partnerships and marriages, including ordinands and clergy in a Church where opinion is deeply divided.

The Alliance of some conservative networks within the Church of England has declared its intention to work, just as opponents of the ordination of women did, for a parallel (3rd) Province in England 'with pastoral oversight from bishops who remain faithful to orthodox teaching on marriage and sexuality'. This provincial proposal was rejected prior to the passing of the 1992 legislation because it divided dioceses and the episcopate. In 1992 the division created by law was on the basis of what parishes believed. The current proposal from the Alliance will be based on what it is believed bishops believe.

I have some understanding of the concerns of those who want no change of doctrine. A bishop is asked at their consecration: 'Will you teach the doctrine of Christ as the Church of England has received it, will you refute error and will you hand on entire the faith that is entrusted to you?' But bishops are also asked: 'Will you promote peace and reconciliation in the Church and in the world; and will you strive for the visible unity of the Church?'

In a culture where identity is often created through splitting, polarization, antagonism and antipathy, the task of a bishop in promoting peace and reconciliation is demanding. In a diocese where leadership and catholic traditions of order are contested, the task of a bishop is particularly demanding. But I have experienced in our diocesan discussions on *Living in Love and Faith* that there is for most a yearning perhaps as strong as a calling to hold together. The diocese is practised in that: its social geography pulls us apart. Our mutual and prayerful affection draws us together. Reception is a way of life as we listen to those with very different experiences in Swindon as well as Bristol, the Cotswold villages, as well as urban priority communities, growing churches, and those with few worshippers.

More than that, across the diocese of the South West the bishops, who hold a range of views on sexual identity and same-sex marriage, have agreed that we will work together to continue to trust one another and to provide care and a voice both for those who believe that sexual relationships between those of the same sex are inherently sinful, and those who yearn to celebrate those relationships. We will work at the consequence of that for ordinands and clergy, creating both legal and sacramental care. In the terms of the Five Guiding Principles, applied to same-sex relating, we will support the first three principles but not the creation of separate structures or enclaves. It is these that have demeaned women and will demean LGBTIQI+ folk who have served – and continue to – the Church with such faithful, gracious and generous love and who, because of their marginalization, find themselves demeaned and their safety at risk. We know we hold the tension inherent in disagreement. We will continue to build bridges, not walls.

We do that for the sake of the world that God loves so much. During the riots of the summer of 2024 there was a remarkable evening when the city of Bristol was again under threat, with a focus on those we welcome as a City of Sanctuary, and alongside them Muslims and anyone seen as black or brown. The local parish, with its longstanding commitment to the whole community, did a prayer walk, just a dozen or so people engaging with those boarding up their businesses who were so afraid. The next night they were joined, as one journalist put it, by folk from all the tribes of Bristol, all those so often divided by politics, race, faith, age and class, standing quietly in the street to resist those who would divide us. Bristol is our common home.

The Diocese of Bristol is learning how it can receive the perspectives of those who disagree and create a common house of welcome and a place of mutual respect, regard and hope.

As Pope John XXIII put it, 'when we come to be judged we shall not be asked if we have achieved unity. We shall be asked if we have worked and prayed and suffered for unity.'

Note

1 The quadruple lock is part of the Marriage (Same Sex Couples) Act 2013, which protects religious freedom and ensures that religious organizations can act in accordance with their beliefs. It decrees that the governing body of the religious organization must explicitly consent to perform same-sex marriages; that the individual minister must be willing to conduct the marriage; that the ceremony must occur in a place of worship that has been registered for same-sex marriages; and that no religious organization or individual minister can be forced to perform same-sex marriages or allow their premises to be used for this purpose.

PART 5

Experience and Conscience

9

Sex Is Not a Dirty Thing: Living in Love and Faith with Maude Royden

HELEN KING

'Sex is not a dirty thing,' wrote the suffragist and campaigner for women's ministry, Agnes Maude Royden, in the preface to the 1922 American edition of her book *Sex and Common-Sense*: 'Passion is essentially noble and those who are incapable of it are the weaker, not the stronger.'[1] Although she was best known as a campaigner for women's suffrage, a pacifist and a preacher, Royden's views on sex, love and passion repay our study today, a century on, particularly in the context of Living in Love and Faith (LLF), the project started by the Church of England in 2017 after the failure of General Synod to 'take note' of a report from the House of Bishops. That project continues, very slowly, and the House has still not agreed whether clergy are allowed to be in same-sex marriages; same-sex civil partnerships are permitted, because of the notion that sex does not happen in those partnerships. For the conservative evangelical wing of the Church of England, heterosexual activity outside straight marriage, as well as sex between partners who identify as the same sex, remains 'a dirty thing'.

Royden was of course partly a product of her time: women's suffrage, the aftermath of World War One meaning there were 'surplus' women, and the Church of England's attempts to reach agreement around contraception and divorce. How could she be anything else? Sue Morgan has, however, correctly characterized

Royden's own beliefs about sexuality as 'highly individual and contentious'.[2] Today, some in the Church of England believe that marriage is a sacrament: others don't. The Faith and Order Commission has been asked by the House of Bishops to explore this. Royden regarded sex as a sacrament, but did not see marriage itself as the basis of this sacramental relationship.[3] Promiscuity, 'The casual connection of a man and a woman who like each other', was for her not as much of a problem as prostitution.[4]

I became interested in Royden's life and relationships in the context of the disputed *Prayers of Love and Faith*, commended by the bishops in December 2023 for use with same-sex couples in existing regular church services; the *Prayers* are still not allowed in 'stand-alone' services for fear that such services would look like straight marriages. There is a parallel between the Living in Love and Faith (LLF) project and the Committee on Women and the Church, established as part of the 1916 National Mission of Repentance and Hope. Maude Royden was scathing about the work of this Committee, because it was 'for research only – not to recommend action'.[5] The LLF project had a similarly limited remit, although the main book published from its years of work did recognize that, where same-sex relationships were concerned, 'decisions in several interconnected areas need to be made with some urgency'.[6] The Church of England, however, defines 'urgency' in its own way.

The only 'fruit' of LLF currently to fall from the tree that was its original logo is the published resource: *Prayers of Love and Faith*.[7] Yet this opens not with material to use with a same-sex couple in a civil partnership or civil marriage, but with some suggestions for marking a 'covenanted friendship'.[8] I was involved in writing the LLF resources from 2017 but although such relationships feature in passing there – with a reference to David and Jonathan, men who were both married, with the nature of their own relationship unclear[9] – I have no recollection of any discussion as to why anyone would want to enter such a covenant today. Is the intention to help those in a church in which sharing a house and a life with a friend is suspected of being sexual, with the covenant a way of dismissing such suspicions? As a member of General Synod and of one of the many working groups set up to discuss using the *Prayers*, I have heard the questions that this section raises: for example, taking up the reference to David and Jonathan, could someone in a marriage also be in a covenanted friendship? Would their spouse have to agree?

It is Royden's complex relationships that show these *Prayers*, and much else in our current discussions of people's lives, for the travesty that they are. As Royden wrote, 'We had not enough knowledge of life or of the human heart to guess of what it is capable in love nor how many ways there are of loving.'[10] Her life challenges all the neat assumptions we bring to these discussions of real people and their relationships.

Before looking at Royden's life in more detail, let's pause to think about what we mean by 'sex'. You can hear the deep breath being taken when, at the end of Chapter 12, the *Living in Love and Faith* book acknowledges that 'we need to talk about sex'.[11] Every so often, somebody speaking in a Synod debate or posing a formal question to the Questions sessions asks what exactly we are talking about here, but the request is inevitably dismissed as prurient, or because 'we all know' what it means. Do we? Although we may acknowledge that couples coming to their priest to discuss marriage are almost always already living together, 'sex' is supposedly only for married couples. A further area of cognitive dissonance today is that the Church of England grants Permission to Officiate to clergy in same-sex civil partnerships, but not to those in same-sex marriages, because it is trying to claim not only that sex is for marriage but also that no sex takes place outside marriages. But if, as is often implied, 'sex' means only penis-in-vagina intercourse, then nothing that happens in a same-sex relationship can possibly count as 'sex'. Logically, this should mean that lesbian and gay people can do what they like and it's no concern of the Church because it isn't 'sex'. And, if 'sex' means penis-in-vagina, then same-sex marriage becomes logically impossible, because there can't be sex if you are not heterosexual.

And there are yet more problems with the implied definition in which only penis-in-vagina counts as 'sex'. What about other orifices, let alone other physical expressions of love? The *Living in Love and Faith* book at least challenged the idea that anal sex was 'largely a gay male phenomenon'.[12] As for oral sex, by the mid-1980s it was increasingly seen as an act that did not end one's virginity,[13] and didn't count as infidelity, as in Bill Clinton's insistence that 'I did not have sexual relations with that woman'.[14] I remember hearing the wife of a prominent clergyman saying that she was very glad that, in her day – this would be the 1970s – Christians were not supposed to 'have sex' before marriage, as that gave her and her husband-to-be the opportunity to explore various enjoyable activities that they may otherwise never have discovered – and I don't think she meant walks in the countryside.

The focus on penis-in-vagina fails to take account of so many experiences of lesbian, gay and straight relationships. It also leads to the long history of focusing on the dubious membrane of the hymen as all that counts, and to the notion of 'technical virginity', as in the coming-of-age comedy *Clueless* (1995): 'Dionne's virginity went from technical to non-existent.'[15] Faith groups have come up with yet more categories such as 'secondary virginity', used for someone who chooses to abstain after previous sexual activity.[16]

Such narrow views of human relationships are illuminated by Maude Royden's experience. Her name was largely forgotten until Sheila Fletcher's 1989 biography, followed from 2010 by a succession of articles. The first woman to preach in the Church of England, Royden had previously been appointed as Assistant Pastor to the Congregational City Temple in Holborn in 1917, with more than 2,600 attending her first sermon there.[17] Then, with Percy Dearmer, she set up the Guildhouse Fellowship in Ecclestone Square in 1920. In 1921, she preached at St Botolph's Bishopsgate, in the church itself rather than in the Parish Room, for the Three Hours Service on Good Friday. St Botolph's was significant because the man Royden had loved since 1901, the Revd George William Hudson Shaw, had been appointed Rector there in 1912 and she was taking part in services in other ways, such as reading the lessons.[18]

Shaw and Royden had met in Oxford while she was having a crisis of faith in which she had considered crossing over to Rome. He was clearly an ally for a woman who felt called to preach, as he was horrified by the Church of England's official position on women, writing when he was still a curate that 'Whether I shall retain my Orders in this respectability-ridden, comfortable, damnable Establishment is more than I can say.'[19]

Working within a postwar 'reconfiguring [of] gender relations in terms of mutual intimacy rather than sexual antagonism',[20] Royden's sermons at the Guildhouse looked for a new 'morality of sex' which both responded to, and informed, secular morality.[21] Her book *Sex and Common-Sense*, first published in the UK, based on her sermons, set her 'within a powerful historical tradition of Christian women speaking out on sex' as authors of self-help and marriage advice manuals.[22] She invited questions after these sermons, modifying the text of successive editions of the book in response to these. Her theology of sex as sacrament challenged the long history of 'the heresy of despising the female body'.[23]

Royden noted the undercurrent of fear of women's bodies that lay behind claims that 'some men are afraid of being sexually excited if they are addressed by a woman-preacher'.[24] None of this, of course, is a feature only of the early twentieth century. Eva's Call, the community artwork created at Cuddesdon in 2018, in which women ordinands and priests recorded what had been said to them, included 'Even more gorgeous than her pictures', 'You're far too pretty to be a vicar' and 'You must tie up your hair when you preside, it makes you look more neutral.'[25]

Yet Royden's contributions to developing the roles open to women in the Church of England existed alongside a complex private life which until recently was less likely to be mentioned – it was entirely ignored by Arthur Downing in 1984 – even though she chose to make that very public indeed by publishing in 1947 *A Threefold Cord*, an account of her long relationship with Shaw and his second wife – and cousin – Effie. The then-Bishop of Rochester, Christopher Chevasse, advised against publishing it because 'It may incite some who have an affair to go on with it – on your recommendation; but without your and his background and Christian faith to uphold them.'[26] And that was the point; while describing a deep and passionate relationship, Royden was not recommending sex outside marriage. But where, for her, would the barriers be? In the correspondence Royden received after publication, a Miss Pickard wrote: 'I cannot quite realise where to place the physical boundary of passionate love', to which Royden replied: 'while you ... long to express that love on the physical as well as the mental and spiritual planes you must never do so ... nor must you allow your thoughts to dwell on what is forbidden'.[27]

She lived with Shaw and his wife, on and off, at one point in adjacent houses. She expressed her love for both, telling her readers that she and Hudson Shaw 'loved each other at first sight' in 1901, although it took them time to realize this.[28] As for Effie – 'Dear, strange, enchanting Effie!' – 'I fell in love with her, too, at first sight ... If she had not loved me and I her, what happened afterwards would have been impossible.'[29] She described how Effie – who was terrified of childbirth, did not want to be pregnant, and never had sex with her husband after the birth of their son and her subsequent breakdown[30] – thoroughly approved of Shaw's passion for her; Royden compared Effie to Shelley, writing that 'she had not his unorthodox standards of sexual behaviour, but she was utterly without possessiveness'.[31] Effie 'did not wish her husband and her friend to transgress their moral standards or hers: she did want us to have all that was possible for us – not love only, but passionate love'.[32] It was understood that this could never be consummated in Effie's lifetime, but Effie suggested they should marry after her death[33] – and they did, in 1944 when Maude was 68 and Shaw 85, two months before his death. The title page of *A Threefold Cord* reads 'by Maude Royden (Mrs Hudson Shaw)'.

What do we make of this relationship? The review in the *Manchester Guardian* of 8 December 1947 suggested that the book 'if written at all it should have been printed for private circulation'. Falby called it 'a "three-cornered" platonic yet passionate relationship', a 'chaste passion';[34] Morgan described it as 'passionate but celibate';[35] Dixon called it a 'complicated relationship'.[36] Is it a superb example of how only marital relationships can be sexual? The dynamics of this group were complex, with Royden and Effie often ganging up to laugh at Shaw. Effie called Royden 'child' and the two women called Shaw 'the Man'.[37]

It is clear that Shaw found it very difficult to have a passionate relationship with Maude without expressing it sexually. She wrote that 'to him passion's fulfilment was most literally a sacrament' as '"the outward and visible sign of an inward and spiritual love"'.[38] The lack of physical expression in his relationship with his wife pained him but he respected it, telling Royden more than once that it was 'the most dreadful thing that could happen to a man to find that that sacrament, for whose sake he had kept his body as clean as a child's, was to his wife merely "a concession to his lower nature"'.[39] As a married man, he could never have 'fulfilment' from Royden;[40] there was always 'the strain of incompletion'[41] so, she writes, 'we never had a "guilty secret" to keep'.[42] For her part, Royden was quite clear that women feel passion too and that to think 'that women suffer nothing or little by the unsatisfaction of the sex side of their nature' was an 'imbecile assumption'.[43]

Are we to assume that their relationship was never physical? This brings us back to the 'what is sex?' question. What about touch: a hug, a kiss? In 1918, in a sermon at the City Temple, she asked, 'Should we not think it a strange kind of love which never wanted ... even to touch the body of a friend or a lover? ... I am speaking now [not] only of the love of sex ... there is a physical side to every kind of love.'[44] Royden later reminisced about some special days out with Shaw, driving to the woods, boating, picnics and talking: always talking.[45] While she destroyed most of his letters, she kept some, including those in which he wrote to her, 'But I had such joy and comfort on Thursday! A lovely hour!' and 'What you gave me was ours though I had not dared to dream of the lovely, lovely gift.'[46] Three years after her marriage, and at the age of 71, she was writing about lesbian mutual masturbation and its potential for an orgasm 'similar to that which is the culmination of ordinary sexual intercourse between persons of different sexes'.[47]

For people living in this period, what they could do was of course constrained by not wanting to risk pregnancy. Royden writes about contraception – as significant a topic of church disagreement then as same-sex marriage is today – and its inevitable failures; the reason why Effie, terrified of pregnancy, had still become pregnant. Royden supported contraception, although also noting that 'some of the noblest, happiest and most romantic marriages I know base their control of conception not on contraceptives but on abstinence. They are not prigs, they are not asexual, they do not drift apart, and they have no harsh criticism to make on those who have decided otherwise. These are facts, and it is useless to ignore them. On the other hand, it is equally true that sometimes such an attempt at self-control leads to nervous strain, irritability and alienation. These also are facts.'[48] While she was honest about the emotional strain of living with Shaw, Royden strongly supported female celibacy.[49] Although she invited Dora Russell – who supported premarital sex – to speak at the Guildhouse in 1927, Royden thought that Russell placed too much weight on individualism.[50]

Last year, Grove Books published the pamphlet *Three or More*. Written by a member of 'Living Out', a group of people who would call themselves 'same-sex attracted' but who choose either abstinence or marriage to an opposite-sex partner, this is just one example of the way in which those opposed to same-sex physical relationships (whatever that means) use the scare tactics of suggesting such relationships are merely the precursor to polyamory, at the very least. The message is 'What can seem surprising now could soon seem unremarkable.'[51]

The past, I suggest, is even more surprising. Maude Royden and Hudson Shaw were clear that they had a passionate relationship that could not be expressed in penis-in-vagina intercourse. For Andrew Bunt – who may well have never heard of them, and in any case would ignore them because their lives undermine his central argument about this, all being post-Pill and 'now' – relationships of the kind they had with each other and with Effie count as polyamorous, even if they are not 'sexually intimate', and so should be rejected. Bunt lists, as if to control, all the terms for such relationships: throuple, vee, metamours, nesting relationship,[52] describing such relationships as not 'morally acceptable to God'.[53] Yet what Maude Royden and Hudson Shaw had was love, and 'passionate love', without full sexual intercourse. They negotiated this according to their beliefs, without judging those who made other choices. To label their emotionally passionate relationship 'polyamorous' seems to miss the point entirely. By the 1947 edition of *Sex and Common-Sense* Royden was writing that sex is 'a lovely thing, lovely, in itself and even if no children are created by it'.[54] We need to accept more positive evaluations of the body and of sex, and to resist the 'respectability-ridden, comfortable, damnable Establishment' with its tendency to put the richness of human relationships into neat boxes labelled 'God's plan' and 'not God's plan'.

Notes

1 Maude Royden, 1922, *Sex and Common-Sense*, New York and London: G. P. Putnam's and Sons, pp. 3–4.

2 Sue Morgan, 'A "feminist conspiracy": Maude Royden, women's ministry and the British press, 1916–1921', *Women's History Review*, 22.5 (2013), p. 779.

3 Alison Falby, 'Maude Royden's sacramental theology of sex and love', *Anglican and Episcopal History*, 79.2 (2010), pp. 125, 133–4.

4 Sheila Fletcher, 1989, *Maude Royden: A Life*, Oxford: Blackwell, p. 232.

5 Morgan, 'A "feminist conspiracy"', p. 787.

6 *Living in Love and Faith: Christian Teaching and Learning about Identity, Sexuality, Relationships and Marriage*, 2020, London: Church House Publishing, p. 422.

7 Helen King, 'Seeing the tree in the woods', in *Shared Conversations*, https://shared-conversations.com/2018/07/08/seeing-the-tree-in-the-woods/ (accessed 7.03.25).

8 See https://www.churchofengland.org/sites/default/files/2023-12/prayers-of-love-and-faith.pdf (accessed 7.03.25).

9 *Living in Love and Faith*, pp. 181–2.

10 Maude Royden, 1947, *A Threefold Cord*, London: Victor Gollancz, p. 12.

11 *Living in Love and Faith*, p. 252.

12 *Living in Love and Faith*, p. 115.
13 Laura M. Carpenter, 2005, *Virginity Lost: An Intimate Portrait of First Sexual Experiences*, New York: New York University Press, pp. 40–1.
14 Helen King, 2024, *Immaculate Forms: Uncovering the History of Women's Bodies*, London: Profile Books/Wellcome Collection, p. 204.
15 King, *Immaculate Forms*, p. 268.
16 King, *Immaculate Forms*, pp. 271–2.
17 Morgan, 'A "feminist conspiracy"', p. 788.
18 Fletcher, *Maude Royden: A Life*, pp. 177–8.
19 Fletcher, *Maude Royden: A Life*, p. 180.
20 Sue Morgan, '"Sex and common-sense": Maude Royden, religion, and modern sexuality', *Journal of British Studies*, 52.1 (2013), p. 162.
21 Morgan, '"Sex and common-sense"', p. 163.
22 Morgan, '"Sex and common-sense"', p. 158.
23 Revd C. Dunkley, ed., 1913, *Official Report of the Church Congress held at Southampton, September 28, 29 and 30 October 1–3 1913*, London: Church Congress, p. 306, cited in Morgan, '"Sex and common-sense"', p. 164.
24 Maude Royden, 1947, *Sex and Commonsense*, Hurst and Blackett, p. 157; Morgan, '"Sex and common-sense"', p. 161.
25 See https://artsrcc.wordpress.com/2018/03/02/evas-call/ (accessed 7.03.25).
26 Fletcher, *Maude Royden: A Life*, p. 279.
27 Fletcher, *Maude Royden: A Life*, p. 280.
28 Royden, *A Threefold Cord*, p. 9.
29 Royden, *A Threefold Cord*, p. 15.
30 Fletcher, *Maude Royden: A Life*, p. 51.
31 Royden, *A Threefold Cord*, p. 22.
32 Royden, *A Threefold Cord*, p. 27.
33 Royden, *A Threefold Cord*, p. 29.
34 Falby, 'Maude Royden's sacramental theology of sex and love', pp. 128, 142.
35 Morgan, '"Sex and common-sense"', p. 159.
36 Joy Dixon, 'Maude Royden (1876–1956) and the "Sacrament of Love"', *Modern Believing*, 64.4 (2023), p. 407.
37 Royden, *A Threefold Cord*, p. 12; Fletcher, *Maude Royden: A Life*, p. 57.
38 Royden, *A Threefold Cord*, p. 27.
39 Royden, *A Threefold Cord*, pp. 28–9.
40 Royden, *A Threefold Cord*, p. 28.
41 Royden, *A Threefold Cord*, p. 57.
42 Royden, *A Threefold Cord*, p. 29.

43 Royden, *Sex and Common-Sense*, p. 9.
44 Fletcher, *Maude Royden: A Life*, p. 223.
45 Fletcher, *Maude Royden: A Life*, p. 229.
46 Royden, *A Threefold Cord*, p. 75.
47 Morgan, '"Sex and common-sense"', p. 174.
48 Royden, *Sex and Common-Sense*, p. 73.
49 Morgan, '"Sex and common-sense"', p. 166.
50 Morgan, '"Sex and common-sense"', p. 168.
51 Andrew Bunt, 2024, *Three or More: Reflections on Polyamory and Consensual Non-monogamy*, Cambridge: Grove Books, p. 3.
52 Bunt, *Three or More*, p. 4.
53 Bunt, *Three or More*, p. 6.
54 Royden, 1947, *Sex and Commonsense*, p. 102.

10

Time for Change

GARETH WARDELL

Let me begin with a disclaimer. I'm neither a 'leading Anglican', nor a theologian. I'm simply a vicar whose life has been impacted by the homophobia and indecision that has characterized the Church's approach to same-sex relationships for too long. What follows is my own story and some brief reflections on this issue, in the hope that this may help to inform debate and accelerate the move to change.

I was raised in a fairly traditional, middle-class English background, where people didn't talk much about sexuality. My father was public school and Oxbridge educated, but my parents were committed to state education, so when I failed my 11+ I ended up being sent to what was then called a secondary modern school on a fairly rough social housing estate, several miles from home. I was a sensitive, artistic child with somewhat effeminate gestures – mannerisms that were accentuated when I was frightened – so I became an obvious target for bullying and physical abuse. I realized quickly the importance of trying to blend in and not attract attention. In the family home we spoke received pronunciation, but in a matter of weeks I'd learnt to speak with a fluent 'saaff-east London' accent. This wasn't affectation, it was an essential survival technique! I mention this because I think it's a helpful metaphor for the way many gay people live their lives in a straight person's world. Having to change to be acceptable to others is a daily experience, especially for those who grow up as part of a conservative evangelical milieu.

As I became aware of my emerging sexual feelings, I wanted

to find out why I felt as I did. I remember going to the school library to look up the word 'homosexual' in an encyclopedia – making sure no one saw me; this wasn't difficult as no one went to the library in my school! But it wasn't a lot of help. What did help was that, at 13, I made a commitment to Christ at a local evangelistic event. I always felt loved and accepted by my local church, but it was a real blow to my confidence some time later when I heard a preacher at another event describe homosexuals as an abomination destined for hell, and 'a stench in the nostrils of God'! I remember being overcome with panic and pleading with God to change or 'heal' me. Bullying was a daily occurrence at school and my spectacles were frequently broken. An abiding memory is of those occasions when I would find myself cornered and lying curled-up in a foetal position, in the playground or in our local shopping precinct, surrounded by a group of older boys who were kicking me repeatedly. I mention this not to garner sympathy, but because it's part of my story and I think it's important to understand 'homophobic abuse' isn't just another tiresome concept dreamed up by the *Guardian*-reading, tofu-eating, wokerati – it's real and very frightening, especially when you're only 12 or 13. Indeed, surviving secondary education was probably the best possible preparation for my subsequent career working in war zones … but I'm getting a bit ahead of myself.

Despite having failed my 11+, by the time of A levels I achieved enough academic success to get into university where, aged 19, I spoke about my orientation for the first time in my life to one of the university chaplains. It was also at university, as an active member of the Christian Union, that I had the first experience of well-meaning people praying for me to be delivered from homosexuality or, as they put it, 'to rebuke the demon of homosexuality and command it to leave me, in the name of Jesus'. I find this kind of prayer, and the theology that underpins it, somewhat problematic. How do you think it feels to be told the strong feelings you have, which are likely to be lifelong, are evidence of demonic possession? It simply isn't possible to 'cast out' something that is an inextricable component of a person's personality without doing violence to the integrity of their being. But that didn't stop people trying, nor did it prevent me from colluding with their efforts. I think the critical issue is whether the Church believes LGBTQ+ people to be fearfully and wonderfully made, as God intended, or whether we are seen, and encouraged to see ourselves, as 'intrinsically disordered'.

Some 50 years ago, attempts were made to 'cure' gay people through what was called 'aversion therapy', which included the use of electric-shock treatment. Some Christians today still advocate what they term 'reparative therapy', which carries the rather patronizing implication that something is broken and in need of repair. Of course, the reality is that in every society, all over the world, throughout history, a small minority of people grow up attracted to their own sex. One might almost imagine this was part of God's plan! An analogy has been made to left-handedness. In most Western societies, we've long since stopped trying to 'correct' children when they begin to show signs of being left-handed. By contrast, when I served as a mission-partner in south Asia, where the left hand is used for lavatory functions, left-handedness was regarded by many as unacceptable. Strong societal and religious disapproval led to some children being smacked or even, occasionally, having their left hand tied behind their back, to try and correct their left-handedness – a kind of aversion therapy, if you will. But the reality is that in all societies, all over the world, throughout history, a small minority of people grow up to be left-handed!

In my early thirties, so deeply internalized was the homophobia I had imbibed, I chose to put myself through a year of counselling/therapy with the express goal of changing my orientation. It made not a scrap of difference – and, believe me, I tried! So I came to the reluctant conclusion that singleness and lifelong celibacy were the only option for someone like me. I spent many years working overseas with a wonderful Christian mission/development agency in some of the toughest places in the world, before returning to the UK for further professional studies; I eventually trained for the priesthood and served as a priest in the Church of England for nearly 20 years, initially in North Yorkshire, latterly in the Diocese of London.

Throughout this time significant changes occurred within the Church on a range of controversial topics, including women's ordination to the priesthood and the episcopacy, and divorce and remarriage in church. For earlier generations there were the issues of slavery and racial segregation, and the use of contraception – all issues that some in the Church argued trenchantly from Scripture, for a particular conservative interpretation, which to a later generation, of equally faithful 'Bible-believing Christians', seemed completely flawed. I was ordained deacon by a divorced bishop, who subsequently remarried – something that would have been unimaginable to previous generations, as would the prospect of female priests and bishops; but the sky didn't fall in, the major splits some argued would result have not occurred and, despite the discomfort some may feel about the compromises made to ensure 'mutual flourishing', the Church has held together and we've agreed to disagree but to still see Christ in one another. So why is the issue of same-sex relationships so different?

During a time of rapid change in British society that has seen the introduction of civil partnerships and same-sex civil marriage, the Church has commissioned various reports and initiatives: the Windsor Report, the Pilling Report, the 'Shared Conversations', Living in Love and Faith, and so forth. But for those of us directly impacted there remains a sense of being talked about while nothing ever changes, and LGBTQ+ lives are just put on hold, collateral damage to be thrown under the proverbial bus – after all, we're only, what, 5 per cent of the population at most, so who cares?

I would argue the time for change has come and the need for change is now urgent because the status quo is cruel, dishonest and immensely damaging both to individuals and families and to the mission of the Church. Paul commends his hearers to a life of celibacy but recognizes that that is too difficult a message for many of his listeners to hear, so he allows marriage. That same grace is not afforded to us. Apparently, 'it is not good for a man (or woman) to be alone' unless they happen to be gay. I have no difficulty with the idea that some may be called to celibacy – clearly some are, and the Church should honour their calling; but to suggest that celibacy is mandated for an entire group of people simply because they happen to be, for example: left-handed, have green eyes, or be gay, seems bizarre.

Far more significant is the message given to vulnerable people that says such an integral part of their identity is sinful, and therefore their desires are sinful. Readers may recall the tragic case of Lizzie Lowe who internalized that message and felt the only way out was to take her own life. Over the years I have been contacted by a number of parents I studied and served with, both in the UK and overseas, whose children were experiencing suicidal thoughts over this issue and the conservative (some would say 'toxic') theology of churches that have literally poisoned the young person's mind. This is a serious missional issue, both for the young people affected, but also for other young people repelled by what they see as homophobia – which they place in the same category as racism and sexism.

Pastoral situations often help to focus the mind, so to those with doubts about whether the Church should bless same-sex marriages, let me tell you about my friends Peter and his husband David.[1] They've been together for over 25 years. Throughout this time, they've been actively involved in their parish church, where Peter was a churchwarden for many years. Some years ago they adopted two boys, birth-siblings, who had been spectacularly failed by their, presumably heterosexual, birth parents. It's been a tough journey, and at the time of their adoption there weren't many people willing to take the boys on as they came with a lot of emotional baggage; but they're now thriving and, for what it's worth, they show every sign of being thoroughly heterosexual – so apparently being gay isn't something you can catch! Who knew? They were baptized, attended Sunday school, and the church youth group that Peter and David helped to run and, when they were old enough, they were confirmed. They're a family and everyone in their village and their local community recognizes them as a family. It seems to me they are already being blessed by God and are unquestionably a blessing to others.

But are they a real family or a fake family? Are they a sinful family? If a family like this turned up at your church, what would you want them to do? Would you encourage them to divorce? Would you want them to hand back their children to social services? What messages would you communicate to those children about God and God's love for them and those who have loved and nurtured them at great cost, when others didn't? Or would you just find it so much easier if they went elsewhere because their presence as a family would pose a subversive challenge to the theology of your church? When I hear the response of some churches to situations like this, I'm reminded of the old joke about a tourist asking for directions and being told, 'Well, if I wanted to get to there, I wouldn't start from here.' The thing is, here is where we are! There are now many thousands of families like this across the UK, including clergy families. How the Church responds to them has direct implications for the mission of the Church.

Something else we need to consider is the outworking of our current approach in the lives of ordinary gay Christians and how the lifelong repression of a person's sexuality, with no possible healthy outlet, may result in unhealthy behaviour that is unsafe for them and others. My observation based on very considerable anecdotal evidence acquired over decades is that, in general, among those evangelicals who are gay and believe Scripture mandates a celibate life, there is a pattern of behaviour characterized by periods of abstinence, followed by a 'sexual fall', or several falls which, by their very nature, tend to be casual or anonymous encounters – because a 'relationship' would be seen as wrong. Such falls are then followed by a period of regret, repentance and further abstinence, until another fall occurs and the whole cycle repeats itself – which it does, again and again and again. Such people normally suffer from an overwhelming sense of guilt, shame, sadness and secrecy, and the feeling that as Christians their lives never quite measure up. It is also important to note that their behaviour may place members of their family at risk, since many of them are in opposite-sex marriages, having been encouraged by their conservative churches to 'pray away the gay' and get married, but who are now living lives of secrecy and denial.

TIME FOR CHANGE

By contrast, those gay Christians I know who believe God affirms their identity tend to be happy, well-adjusted people, who by mid-life are normally in a long-term, faithful relationship – some having been with their partner for 25 years or more. And so perversely and entirely counter-intuitively, I've come to realize that if a person is gay and evangelical in their convictions, their life is more likely to be characterized by promiscuous, risky, anonymous, guilt-inducing sexual behaviour that leaves them feeling sad, lonely and isolated. By contrast, the supposedly more liberal, gay-affirming Christians are the ones more likely to be living lives characterized by loving, stable, faithful monogamy. I appreciate there are exceptions to this rule. I also led an entirely celibate life until my early sixties, albeit not without personal cost, sacrifice and loneliness. But not everyone can; and truth be told, probably not many straight people could either! So when I reflect on some of the pronouncements about gay people emanating from some parts of the Church, I'm reminded of Jesus' words about the Pharisees: 'they do not practise what they teach. They tie up heavy burdens, hard to bear, and lay them on the shoulders of others; but they themselves are unwilling to lift a finger to move them' (Matt. 23.3–4).

To me, one of the great riches of the Anglican Church is its breadth and diversity. I spent much of my life within the evangelical wing of the Church and there is much that I still cherish about the tradition that has shaped and formed my faith. I may disagree with others on this issue, but there is so much more that unites us rather than divides us and I wouldn't dream of separating from the Church of England to which we belong. No clergy should be required to use the Prayers of Love and Faith if this is against their conscience, just as no clergy are required to offer to remarry divorcees. But those of us who wish to do so, or to avail ourselves of prayers of blessing following civil marriage, should not be denied that opportunity because of the conscience of another. Part of being brothers and sisters in Christ together is that we can challenge one another's views while maintaining fellowship, learning to disagree well and seeking to find our way forward together.

Finally ... I began with an account of my own story, so let me return to that briefly. Two years ago, after leading an entirely celibate life for 63 years, I met the man who is now my partner. Were this a Victorian romantic novel, I might end by saying 'Reader: I married him.' But of course I can't because, were I to do so, I would risk losing my licence as a priest, my home and my job. I could enter into a civil partnership, but this may involve the need to be economical with the truth about our relationship, so for now we live in an uncomfortable limbo. So, the decisions the Church makes about whether to allow LGBTQ+ clergy to marry are personal. It's time for this to change.

Note

1 Names have been changed to protect identities.

PART 6

Prayer and Guidance

11

Created in the Image and Likeness of God: Or Are We?

CHARLIE BELL

What does it mean to be a human being?
This is surely the central question for so many of our philosophies, ideologies and religions. For Christians, as for many others seeking to answer it from a religious perspective, then a supplementary question – or, more properly expressed, a preceding question – comes: what can we say about the nature of God, and our relationship with this God? What does it mean to be created in the image and likeness of God, and how does this impact on us in our lives together? How do we live well in our lives as human beings? For what were we made and for whom? To what do we journey and why?

Yet in much of contemporary UK society, religion as an idea has slowly receded into that form of living labelled as quirky or eccentric or – frankly – irrelevant. Yes, we have an established Church, and yes, we have churches on most street corners, but our contribution to societal questions of anthropology and meaning has become increasingly marginalized. In many ways this is no surprise – not only has church attendance plummeted, but so too, on far too many occasions, has the quality of our contribution to the national conversation and the resultant credibility. Our unwillingness to treat those outside the Church as conversation partners, and our determination to keep banging a simplistic drum in the name of 'evangelism', has meant that nobody is really listening any more.

Who can blame them? The Church of England's teaching, such as it is, on moral issues is so often little more than bland truisms or 'thou shalt nots', with all the working left out. Perhaps the most recent example of this decline in serious debate was during the passage of the Marriage (Same Sex Couples) Act 2013, in which the contributions from the House of Bishops appeared to be little more than scaremongering and dog-whistle politics. The Archbishop of Canterbury stated that the Act would 'see marriage "abolished, redefined, and recreated", suggesting that "the idea of a marriage as covenant is diminished. The family in its normal sense, predating the state, and as our base community of society ... is weakened".'[1] Other bishops joined him, with the former Archbishop of Canterbury George Carey arguing that opening marriage to same-sex or same-gender couples would leave marriage more widely in a 'weakened and diminished' state.

In the ten years since, it is hard to argue that this is even remotely the case – instead, what appears to have happened is that people in same-sex, same-gender relationships have simply entered into marriages, with all the joys and challenges any marriage contains. Ten years on, however, it does not appear that the Church has done anything like the reflection it might have done on the reality of these same-sex unions – instead, it has spent much of the time asking whether it might bless such couples or enable clergy to enter into such unions in a dry and abstract way that appears to take almost no notice of the human lives of which it speaks. Still the Church of England remains in a place where forms of abstracted theology (if indeed it is theology, rather than warmed-up outdated sociology) are made use of in place of a poise of listening to the Holy Spirit and looking for what might be happening in the human lives we are called to enrich and enliven.

For all the doom-laden rhetoric of the parliamentary debate, one thing that was missing from the wider Church's response was any serious attempt to justify and explain precisely what the Church understood marriage to be in its essence, and why this was particularly life-giving. In the years since, there have been some attempts to address this failing, yet still the answers on marriage seem endlessly to return to body parts, or reproduction (a better choice of word than procreation, which has a wider meaning). Tenuous links to the two Genesis Creation myths (Gen. 1 and 2), and Jesus' reflection on them (Matt. 19; Mark 10), have been made use of to suggest that Jesus defines marriage as between a man and a woman, which is to do violence to the text, and the intelligence of the reader. Much has been written about what 'the Bible clearly teaches', but this 'clear teaching' rarely moves beyond the peripherals to the central message.

At the heart of the problem, then, is a continued failing to engage with what exactly marriage is – and how this essence speaks to who might form part of it. It is only by addressing this that the Church might be able to get itself out of the hole it continues to dig for itself, both in its internal debates and its engagement with the world outside. Further to this is a failure to engage with what exactly humankind is – how we each relate to God, to the image and likeness of God, and to one another. Marriage, in other words, is not the starting point – it is a reflection of a deeper truth about relationships, love, companionship, covenant, faithfulness, holiness. These are characteristics of a life lived in God that are not only found in marriage, and yet far too often Christian theology appears to suggest that they find their fulfilment only in this kind of relationship.

Not only does this do huge damage to other vocations or ways of life – among them celibacy and singleness – and their potential sacramentality, but our attempted building up of marriage into a form of perfect 'state of being' loads theological import on to it in a way that it cannot support (indeed, it turns an institution into a rod for the back rather than a descriptor of a deeper reality). Marriage, ultimately, remains a bond between two flawed, individual, sinful human beings, and this should not be seen as a threat but rather acknowledged as a reality. It is for this reason that marriages fall apart; that however good the intentions, marriages sometimes 'fail', like other interpersonal relationships. Yet even the language of failure seems to do no justice to the real, lived experience of the Christian journey – to aim for something but for it not to reveal itself is not so much failure as part of the learning to live in a world in which intentions do not always match outcomes, and in which we, as fallible human beings, endlessly know ourselves not to be God and to be in need of freely given forgiveness. There is much to unpack here, yet we spend precious little time engaging with it.

There has been a recognition in recent times that divorce might indeed be the right decision in some cases, yet the Church of England's way of managing divorced and remarried clergy remains entirely unfit for purpose, intrusive and inappropriate. It is, perhaps, a good example of where the Church has refused to follow its theology through to its natural conclusions, leaving it instead at a halfway point in order not to scare the horses. Clergy in such cases are still treated with suspicion, and the divorce is a formal obstacle over which to climb, rather than a pastoral reality with which to engage. For those approaching the Church for remarriage after divorce, still the Church of England uses the phrase 'exceptional circumstances' without any apparent recognition of the absurdity of the phrase.[2] Divorce is still unacceptable – with some softening around the edges if the priest sees fit. It is grudging, and appeals to an ideal that exists only in a fevered imagination. This is hardly a worked-through, consistent or credible theology.

The absurdity becomes clearer when we consider the fact that whatever the Church might say about the theology of marriage, the practical reality of being an established Church that must marry all (opposite-sex) parishioners (and select others) means that this theology has little to no place in the intentions or marriages of the vast majority of those who choose the church as their 'venue' for their wedding day. Of course, that is somewhat inevitable in an established Church, yet perhaps we might learn to be a little humbler when trying to keep same-sex, same-gender couples out of marriage on 'theological grounds'. It is not hard to see why our position comes across as intrinsically homophobic – opposite-sex couples can do whatever they like, but our 'theology' allows us to keep same-sex couples outside. Of course, that suggests that we do indeed have a theology.

CREATED IN THE IMAGE AND LIKENESS OF GOD

This brings us back to that debate in the House of Lords. In the same debate, the Bishop of Leicester spoke of being 'one whose respect for and appreciation of gay clergy is deep and who recognises in them sacrificial lives and fruitful ministries', and who was yet unable to support same-sex marriage. Interestingly, he spoke to his concern that same-sex marriage would 'bring to an end the one major social institution that enshrines ... complementarity' between the sexes, which ultimately highlights the issue that lurks at the centre of much of the debate around marriage – and sexuality in general (however squeamish we might be about the term 'obey').

Are men and women (however defined, itself a topic for further consideration) more different than they are similar? Is there a deep ontological divide that cannot be crossed? Is the love, relating and sexual intimacy between people of the same sex or gender fundamentally different to the love, relating and sexual intimacy between people of the opposite sex or gender? Is there, in other words, one image and likeness of God, variously expressed, or several? Are there first-class versions of this image, and cast-offs – or do we need to fundamentally rethink our approach?

This is not a new topic for the Church. Complementarity – the idea that there really is an unbridgeable divide – has been made use of in debates about women's ordination and the role of women in the home and society. Similarly, the idea of ontological differences between different human beings has been used to demean and dehumanize, perhaps most clearly seen in the racist theologizing that suggested black people were of a different nature to – and therefore subordinate to – their white counterparts.[3] The creation of homosexuality as a 'therapeutic category' (a superficially more acceptable description than the 'intrinsic disorder' of the Roman Catholic catechism) is part and parcel of the same kind of pseudoscientific and pseudotheological enterprise.[4] In each of these cases, the normative – the white, cis-heterosexual male – takes on theological importance, and anyone who is not this normative is somehow different, and lesser. Not only are they different and lesser in human terms, but the most damaging element is that they are claimed, however implicitly, to be lesser in theological – in God's – terms. It is not hard to see how normative theology then flows, is baptized as 'orthodoxy', and is fiercely guarded by those who benefit from its assumptions.

For while these assumptions are frequently then described as facts, they are nothing of the sort – they remain assumptions. Intimacy between people of the same sex or gender is assumed to be different to that between people of the opposite sex or gender, and this assumption is then used as the lens through which to read Scripture or any other sources of authority. The questions that are therefore asked are then coloured by these assumptions, and the answers necessarily follow a particular pattern. Asking the Bible questions that assume black people are different to white people means that the answers you find are already framed in that paradigm. Similarly, asking the Bible questions that assume same-sex relationships are inherently different to opposite-sex relationships inevitably does the same. In other words, when we ask 'what does the Bible have to say about same-sex relationships?', we have already assumed that they are different in nature from other relationships – so our questioning of Scripture is already biased.

This is the issue the Church of England has faced when addressing issues of marriage. We continue to assume that same-sex relationships are fundamentally different to opposite-sex ones, and therefore we approach the topic in a way that cements in this difference. Our conversations around reproduction (as a necessary part of marriage) follow this predictable format. Consequently, we are able to ignore the fact that many opposite-sex pairings (and, indeed, sexual acts) are not open to reproduction in a similar manner to same-sex pairings by first asserting that the fact that it is a male-female relationship is of utmost importance. Yet why should this be the case? If a couple is unable to conceive through penile-vaginal sexual intercourse, then why should it matter if this couple is opposite-sex or same-sex? The outcome in both cases is the same – and neither couple will be reproducing sexually. If we were to approach it from this perspective, then we might be more willing to see the fact that our determination to keep same-sex couples out of marriage appears to be rather more homophobic than principled.

This returns us to those Genesis myths and our approach to Scripture – are these passages here saying that 'one-flesh-ness' can only be between men and women, or are they here to speak about how human beings relate to one another? There is no doubt that there are deeply complementarian themes found in some of the writing of Scripture – we might, for example, think of the passages in the Epistles about wives obeying husbands (alongside slaves obeying masters in Eph. 5) or women not speaking in church (1 Cor. 14). The questions we need to be asking are: first, how those passages relate to the rest of Scripture; second, how they relate to our wider church life and interpretation (it is fascinating, for example, to see women bishops so strident in their opposition to same-sex marriage based on passages so often used to question their validity as bishops); third, how contemporary scientific and sociological analysis might enrich our interpretation of Scripture; and fourth, whether these are prescriptive, descriptive, for-all-time pronouncements or contextual statements, and finally what the place of individual scriptural passages are in the wide arc of doctrinal development across the history of the Church.

Doctrinal development is something treated with suspicion by far too many within the Church of England, but however much we might want to pretend that our doctrines are set in stone and immovable, that is simply not true. Marriage, for example, has changed time and again, whether in its meaning, its purpose, its practical outworking, the nature of the covenantal agreement, and the liturgical embodiment of these things. What it means to be married is objectively not the same thing now as it was in many of the preceding centuries of the Church catholic (and before). Many will rejoice in that fact, and yet we appear to be unwilling to follow the increasingly consent-based, covenantal understanding of marriage that builds up the couple, that enables participation in the creative will of God (the truer meaning of procreation), that provides a stable basis for family life, to its natural conclusion; which is to say that it is in the nature of the relating of the couple that marriage is actually found, and not in the peripheries – and certainly not in the particular shape of the genitalia.

If, however, we are willing to do that work, then we find ourselves in a place where – unless we can truly say the relating between opposite-sex couples is different to that between same-sex couples (not least in a post-contraceptive age) – then we might not only find a place for same-sex couples in marriage but might also begin to understand the essence of marriage itself. It is surely this relating that reflects something of God – and it is surely this relating that is the bedrock for the 'goods' of marriage, as variously defined. This is relating at a deeply intimate level – an intimacy that is distinct from, though not perhaps always deeper than, friendship, and an intimacy that usually finds itself expressed in a range of bodily, physical expression. The bodily, physical expression is not somehow separate from this relating or, indeed, that which creates it – the bodily, physical expression of intimacy is bound up with the relating in a way that ebbs and flows, yet which serves to build up that intimacy and the love that sits at the heart of the relationship between the human beings at the centre.

If that distinct intimate relating is indeed the centrepiece of marriage, then it frees us from the need to talk endlessly about body parts and what is permitted to go where, when and how, and instead ask how that intimate relating is best curated in a relationship that embodies the distinctive bond of marriage. All of us know that we don't create a marriage on a wedding day – it is a process of holy fellowship that is always in flux, and which, we might hope, continues to grow and flourish, both within the relationship and outwards into the world outside, day after day till death ends it.

We need, therefore, to have more serious conversations about the place of sex within that relationship, and to get beyond the somewhat arbitrary wedding day as the moment that sexual intimacy can begin. It may be that the public witnessing of love that forms a wedding service is the day that some couples will choose as the moment to enter more deeply into intimacy in a sexual way. Yet for others, that will not be the case, and it is hard to find strong theological reasons to object to that. Indeed, it is challenging to find strong theological reasons to object to sexual relations outside of marriage if only on the grounds that there is no neat dividing line between the sexual and the non-sexual. A cursory look at reality will enable us to see this, yet we are so often determined not to engage with the real and instead to engage with what we wish were the case. This will simply not do for those wishing to think theologically.

Finally, a focus on relating will allow us to move beyond the idea that marriage is the be-all and end-all to a position whereby we listen and learn from the multitude of relationships that form the complex web of human interactions: from friendships, to singleness, to community living, to celibacy – even, dare we say, to new forms of living like polyamory and open relationships. Such things need not scare us, but our response to them will only be serious if we build our thinking on rock and not sand. Our failure to do so to date has led us to caricature the lives of others, and in the meantime look less and less credible in our output.

As an established Church, we do still have things to say and hope to offer to a world that remains confused and conflicted. To do so, however, the Church needs to get a grip and engage in explorations and conversations that mark it out as a good faith conversation partner. If we are unwilling to do the work to sharpen up our own thinking and stick with our theological journeying even when it feels new or uncomfortable, then there is no reason for anyone else to listen to us. We have a choice – we can keep saying the same thing in the same way and be ignored, or we can listen and engage with others, enriching the conversation and pointing people back to the image and likeness of the God who we worship. There is little time to lose.

Notes

1 Madeleine Davies, 'Bishops gather in Lords to vote against gay-marriage Bill', *Church Times* (7 June 2013).

2 Church of England, 'Marriage in church after divorce: form and explanatory statement', at https://www.churchofengland.org/sites/default/files/2017-11/MarriageAFTERdivorceFORM.pdf (accessed 07.03.25).

3 Kristopher Norris, 2020, 'The theological origins of white supremacy', in Kristopher Norris, *Witnessing Whiteness: Confronting White Supremacy in the American Church*, Oxford: Oxford University Press, pp. 33–60.

4 Heather White, 2015, *Reforming Sodom: Protestants and the Rise of Gay Rights*, Chapel Hill: University of North Carolina Press.

12

Towards a Unified Theory of Sexual Morality

THEO HOBSON

One hesitates to criticize God, especially in such august company, but when he invented sex did he really know what he was doing? I mean it, sort of: there is something uniquely problematic about this thing, which is in a sense two things: the expression of a stable loving bond, and the almost exact opposite of this too: an anarchic animal urge.

My category heading is 'Prayer and Guidance'. I won't dwell on prayer (some things are even more embarrassing to discuss than sex). My focus is on the Church's core teaching on sex and marriage, and 'guidance' seems like a useful alternative to 'teaching' or 'doctrine' – less didactic, less doctrinaire. I will, after a brief account of the developments of recent decades, ask what sort of guidance is required now.

The Church of England's traditional teaching on sex and marriage is roughly as follows. Marriage good, sex outside of it bad. Since the mid nineteenth century, the meaning of marriage subtly changed with the right to divorce and the rise of women's rights, and many Anglicans gradually began to see the need for a more nuanced, less brittle view of sex. But the old line could still be held, into the mid twentieth century.

The rise of premarital sex was the game-changer. One form of it was hard to oppose: a couple having sex prior to their wedding. Accordingly, it had never been very strictly forbidden – it was accepted in medieval times as 'espousal', and no one has ever been shocked by a shotgun wedding. So when in the 1960s premarital cohabitation became common, even normal, the Church quietly condoned it.

But of course 'premarital sex' does not just refer to a stable young couple, too red-blooded to wait for their wedding night. It also refers to a casual approach to sex, the new culture of promiscuity, enabled by oral contraceptives among other factors; and no rule can draw a clear line between the two. If it is OK for a couple to have sex because they are in love and intending to marry, is it OK for a couple to have sex because they are in love, though not ready to think about marriage? Is it OK for a couple to have sex on a first date because it might open the door to love and commitment? In practice, it became normal for a young person to have one or two serious relationships before marrying, as well as a few briefer dalliances, or more than a few. How on earth was the Church to address this new landscape? A lot of toothpaste was out of the tube. To return to our theme, what sort of *guidance* could the Church now offer people?

It stuck with the traditional teaching, but it became hollowed out, impossible to take seriously. Or maybe it became more of an unrealistic ideal than a practical rule. But maybe this didn't matter. 'Unrealistic' is not really a fault in Christian teaching – did not Jesus command us to be perfect?

Then came homosexuality. Well, it was already there, but it only commanded real attention from the mid-1970s. It became apparent, at least to some, that there might be a problem with the old teaching, a more serious problem than it being a bit unrealistic. In relation to homosexuality, the censure of sex outside of marriage had teeth. It condemned for life a particular category of person. What did gay Christians, and liberal sympathizers, propose? There seemed no real plan, except to argue for toleration, and wait for attitudes to change.

I want to suggest that this was pretty disastrous, this vagueness within liberal Anglican opinion. There was no will to admit the scale of the problem: that a comprehensive rethink on sex and marriage was needed – in response to the various shifts of recent decades, not just homosexuality. Instead, the assumption

TOWARDS A UNIFIED THEORY OF SEXUAL MORALITY

emerged that the Church's teaching on sex and marriage was still more or less fit for purpose, *but did not apply to homosexuals*. In effect, they should be treated as a different category of Christian. Because they cannot marry, let them have a sort of exemption from the general rule, the monogamous ideal, let them work out their own sexual salvation.

This was an improvement on condemning them, but it was deeply dubious theology. In fact, it did condemn them – to a separate lawless category. It can't be right to say that a certain group is not included in a central Christian teaching. There was a need for a new unified theory of Christian sexual morality, but liberals baulked at this, sensing the magnitude of the undertaking. (The conservative position is more theologically serious, in this respect: it refuses to exempt homosexuals from the general rule.)

We have entered complex and contentious territory. The complexity relates to the question of the otherness of gay culture, its otherness from mainstream sexual morality. Is this otherness intrinsic to homosexuality, or a secondary aspect of gay culture that developed in response to marginalization and persecution? There's obviously no simple answer, to put it mildly. But unless this question is asked, in a sustained and profound way, evasion reigns.

When it emerged from the shadows in the late nineteenth century, homosexuality obviously had an aura of otherness, marginality, dissent from mainstream sexual culture. This was in response to its persecution, of course – but there was also an impulse to make a virtue of its difference. Even before Oscar Wilde, there was a tradition of claiming an affinity with Socrates and other ancients, and also modern geniuses including Shakespeare. And there was also a Christian aspect to this, evident in Oscar Wilde's *De Profundis*: a claim of spiritual sensitivity and vulnerability, with references to exclusion, martyrdom. This tradition of claiming rarefied aesthetic and spiritual otherness blurred with the less highfalutin impulse to dissent from mainstream sexual morality, to defy assumptions about the need to confine sex to long-term committed relationships.

Even in the late twentieth century, the assumption continued that homosexuality was morally different, that the mainstream sexual morality narrative did not apply to it. In the decades following decriminalization, hardly anyone campaigned for the legal recognition of gay unions. Gay marriage still sounded oxymoronic. Progressive opinion, including progressive Christian opinion, affirmed homosexuality *in its otherness*, including its otherness from hetero-normative moral assumptions.

It is arguable that some gay Anglicans intensified the problem of 'separate development', by implying that their experience gave them special insight into major Christian themes: suffering persecution, being seen as unclean, defiance of the 'law', in favour of the inner meaning of the gospel (love), rejecting shame, in favour of the goodness of bodily creation, incarnation.

But they were in an impossible position. Had gay Anglicans strongly argued for the full recognition of same-sex unions, around 1990, this would have been seen as more threatening to traditional Christian teaching than their vague appeal to be tolerated in their otherness.

The Church's document of 1991, *Issues in Human Sexuality*, was rather contradictory. It tried, or half-tried, to address the problem of homosexual Christians' exclusion from mainstream sexual morality. The Church should encourage them in marriage-like fidelity (or abstinence), it said, though it cannot affirm their unions. But gay *clergy* should not feel free to take the marriage-like fidelity option. It is little surprise that many gay clergy continued to feel beyond the pale.

Jeffrey John, in *Permanent, Faithful, Stable* (1993), was clear that a fuller affirmation of homosexual monogamy was the only way out of the mounting crisis; and he was clear that this affirmation must entail a negation. The book criticizes some gay Christians for their 'uncritical acceptance of the tenets of secular sexual liberationism ... they leave gay people with no moral structure or emotionally secure and sexually healthy lives'.[1] He approvingly quotes the gay Catholic writer Andrew Sullivan, criticizing gay activists' response to the AIDS crisis: 'saving lives was less important than saving a culture of "promiscuity as a collective way of life"'.² John grasps the nettle more directly than any heterosexual writer is likely to: 'We need to counter the idea that promiscuous gay sex is somehow more excusable than promiscuous heterosexual sex, or that it is a morally irrelevant expression of biological need ("little more than sneezing", as I once heard it described).'³

Jeffrey John's short book is important for another reason. Its advocacy of same-sex unions entails a deconstruction of marriage. Instead of just accepting marriage's authority, we have to ask what is Christianly good about it. It is good because it enshrines mutual love and fidelity. These things can exist outside of marriage too, in gay relationships. So Christians should affirm gay relationships. In other words, the goodness of marriage is not intrinsic and axiomatic but a function of its core content, its essence. Marriage has a *detachable essence.*

John pointed the way out of the crisis. But his message was politely ignored. Few Anglicans wanted to hear about the sacred worth of gay unions, sensing that this was a threat to marriage's aura of intrinsic authority. But also, many gay Anglicans resisted his moralizing about gay culture, which felt too close to the approach of *Issues in Human Sexuality*. This, I suggest, was a major mistake that hindered the debate, one that set it back. Gay Anglicans, and liberals, had an opportunity to form a clear reformist position. Instead, the assumptions of secular identity politics dominated: there must be no criticism of any aspect of gay culture. Also, some gay Anglicans wanted to hold on to the aura of quasi-religious otherness.

Instead of real thinking from liberals, there were a lot of indignant complaints about the Church being prejudiced. And in a sense it did not help that attitudes in wider society shifted and equal marriage came along, for now liberal Anglicans just insisted that it was obvious that the Church should catch up with secular culture, as a matter of simple justice.

But it was not, and is not, obvious. The secular liberal affirmation of homosexuality is really just a matter of toleration. It is two-dimensional compared to the question of whether the Church should affirm it. For example, does one believe that

David Cameron's affirmation of equal marriage means that he would therefore be equally happy if his own son or daughter was homosexual? The three-dimensional affirmation of homosexuality entails confronting this, asking what homosexuality is, caring what it is. The Church is to be congratulated for stalling, for refusing to rush into a two-dimensional affirmation of homosexuality.

What does it mean for Christians to fully affirm homosexuality? For Jeffrey John and Andrew Sullivan, it means that homosexuality should be part of the dominant narrative of sexual morality, which entails judgement on the morally lax side of gay culture, the spurning of monogamy. For other gay Anglicans, it means affirming homosexuality *as it is*, in all its current ambiguity. According to the latter view, homosexuality is partly inclined to monogamy, partly not; it's all part of God's good creation. But surely some aspects of God's good creation must be affirmed discriminatingly. No one suggests that *heterosexuality* should be affirmed undiscriminatingly (except maybe the social media influencer Andrew Tate). The Church does not affirm heterosexuality per se, but heterosexuality as a tradition shaped by monogamy – *tamed* by monogamy, you could say. It seems that some gay Christians overlook this, and seek the affirmation of homosexuality per se, as if it is fundamentally good. But of course this overlooks the fallenness of all sexuality. It is an understandable reaction to the vilification of homosexuality, to want to affirm the *innocence* of this form of sexuality, but it must be contested.

So it's my claim that the paralysis of the last 30 years is not just the result of homophobia in the Church. It is also because of the failure of gay Anglicans, and other liberals, to make their case. They have allowed Jeffrey John's position to be elbowed aside by more strident, less nuanced voices. Because of the sensitive nature of the issue, to focus on examples might seem uncivil. I can only insist that this issue is too important to be evaded, and hope that fellow Anglicans agree.

In *Fathomless Riches, Or How I Went From Pop to Pulpit* (2014), Richard Coles recounts his youthful involvement in a gay subculture where promiscuity was the norm. (He blurs the boundary between lovers and friends: 'We were all sleeping together, even me, though nervously, in the spirit of Walt Whitman's "army of lovers"'.)[4] Then, when his pop career crashes to earth, he finds God, and soon he starts studying theology with a view to getting ordained. The reader presumes that his days of casual sex are over. But, in fact, after a celibate phase he has a less celibate one:

> There followed some months of sexual adventure, and occasionally misadventure, conduct unbecoming of a clergyman, but I was not a clergyman and to those who would think it unbecoming of a Christian I would say yes, but also that this period of adventure allowed me finally [sic] put to rest the persistent and deeply damaging myth of my own undesirability. The glory of God, said St Irenaeus in the first century [sic], is a person fully alive, and while he could not have had in mind late-night lay-by debaucheries at the turn of the twenty-first century, through them I got closer to being fully human than I ever had before. I shared intimacies of the most profound and tender kind with people I would only have passed by in any other place or at any other time ...[5]

Once he is accepted for ordination, no further indiscretions are related. But, as the above passage shows, ordination does not lead him to rethink his attitude to casual sex. He implies that gay people might have a special calling to dissent from bourgeois sexual norms, and that there is Christian value in this dissent; it can be a means of grace. There is a benign anarchism in casual gay sex, a holy rocking of the bourgeois boat. The claim is that gay Christians have *an alternative version of sexual morality*.

Coles's story is interestingly complemented by that of Giles Goddard, as told in his recent book, *Generous Faith*. As a newly ordained priest he was in a same-sex relationship; when it ended he threw himself into the gay party scene. One of his personas was 'sex-fiend ... playing the field like a premier league star'.[6] He expresses sorrow for the hurt he caused people during this time, but avoids saying anything that might sound critical of this form of gay culture. At one point he speaks of his struggle, at this time, to reconcile being a priest with being 'a London gay man'.[7] But there is no critical analysis of the latter identity. The implication is that gay men will naturally let off steam in this way (whether in response to institutional homophobia, or just because it feels natural and harmless, he does not say). Like Coles, he seems to imply that homosexuality has a special relationship with sexual morality, as a result of its exclusion from the mainstream.

This division within gay Anglican culture must be addressed. The case for a unified theory of sexual morality must be asserted, against those implicitly arguing for the moral separatism of homosexuals.

It now seems that the clear majority of bishops advocate the Jeffrey John view, that sex is permissible within stable unions, gay or straight. This shift should have occurred about 20 years earlier, and much of the blame for delay lies with the inept stridency of reformers, their fear of sounding moralistic, of losing their radical edge.

I am pro-reform, but I am also hesitant. I think that the Church should move to the affirmation of equal marriage, but in the right way. The workings have to be right, as in a maths exam. Some tricky issues have to be properly faced, or it will misfire. And this is one of them: we need to admit that the nature and destiny of homosexuality has been unclear. It must be included in the general sexual morality, and not retain an aura of separatism. It must be affirmed as heterosexuality is – as a fallen thing, in need of ordering. It must be subject to the same constraining principle: that sex detached from long-term mutual fidelity is illegitimate.

And there is another issue to be addressed, which I have alluded to throughout my account of recent developments. There must be a new honesty that marriage has been deconstructed, that it no longer has its old automatic authority in Christian sexual morality. It was partly deconstructed by the normality of premarital sex. Then it was more fully and thoughtfully deconstructed by the rise of pro-gay Christian theologians such as Jeffrey John, insisting that stable faithful unions should be affirmed.

TOWARDS A UNIFIED THEORY OF SEXUAL MORALITY

This is a risky argument, because marriage's aura of intrinsic authority has shaped Christian lives, and still does. If the Church edges away from this aura, that is likely to look like a capitulation to our culture's approach to sex. But the risk must be taken. Absolutizing marriage gets in the way, and prevents the Church from issuing meaningful guidance to a young person. Some readers might be smiling at the idea of a young person looking to the Church for guidance on sex. But that's an evasion: 'no one's listening so it doesn't matter what the Church says'. It does matter. Young Anglicans are capable of sensing whether the Church is attempting to address this issue, or whether it is hiding behind empty platitudes. 'No sex outside marriage' is, for the majority of young Anglicans, an empty platitude (only evangelicals see it as a benign rule). In reality, the average young Anglican requires guidance on sex – honest guidance. They want encouragement in their attempt to take sex seriously. They want to resist the conformist flippancy of their peers, the pretence that promiscuity is fine. They want to treat sex as deeply meaningful, but sense that absolutizing marriage is the mark of a narrow subculture, to which they do not belong. It's difficult pursuing that narrow path: why shouldn't the Church offer encouragement, guidance?

So we must drop the rule of 'No sex outside marriage'. We must recognize that most Anglicans have moved to thinking about sexual morality in a new way – thanks to the changes of the 1960s and then the crisis over homosexuality. In practice, the aura of marriage's axiomatic supremacy has ended, and people have begun to think from the ground up, as it were – and we should admit it. Only then can the Church offer credible guidance to people about sex. Only then can it meaningfully discourage promiscuity – and only then can it praise the 'detachable essence' of marriage, mutual fidelity. Yes, there is a risk involved, in the dethroning of an absolute ideal. But honesty has become obligatory: idealism must be reconstructed on the basis of it.

Here is my summary of the new approach:

The Church of England sees sex as God's gift, but remembers that humans are fallen. Sex is God's gift when it expresses love and mutual commitment, and especially when the couple has made a public pledge of lifelong commitment in marriage. Marriage is a human tradition, subject to error and change, and so should not be seen as an absolute mark of divine favour. But this uncertainty is no excuse for contravening its spirit, its essence – mutual fidelity. Sexual activity that resists the logic and orbit of marriage is an anarchic danger that all Christians must shun.

Note the 'all'.

Notes

1 Jeffrey John, 2012, *Permanent, Faithful, Stable*, London: Darton, Longman & Todd, p. 42.
2 John, *Permanent, Faithful, Stable*, quoting Andrew Sullivan, 1998, *Love Undetectable*, London: Chatto and Windus, p. 52.
3 John, *Permanent, Faithful, Stable*, p. 47.
4 Richard Coles, 2014, *Fathomless Riches, Or How I Went From Pop to Pulpit*, London: Weidenfeld and Nicolson, p. 47.
5 Coles, *Fathomless Riches*, p. 225.
6 Giles Goddard, 2024, *Generous Faith: Creating Vibrant Christian Communities*, Norwich: Canterbury Press, p. 46.
7 Goddard, *Generous Faith*, p. 106.

www.ingramcontent.com/pod-product-compliance
Lightning Source LLC
Chambersburg PA
CBHW060609080526
44585CB00013B/749